CW00661493

Grammar Survival for Secondary Teachers

This third edition of *Grammar Survival* brings the content fully up to date with the new National Curriculum and GCSEs, making it current and relevant for all secondary school English teachers.

Grammar Survival for Secondary Teachers combines knowledge about grammar with pedagogical approaches. Each left-hand page sets out the knowledge teachers need about different aspects of grammar, incorporating research evidence where appropriate, and each right-hand page offers practical ideas and methods for teaching it, often in the context of authentic texts to show grammar in action.

This book aims to help pupils become more confident readers and writers, able to make conscious and informed choices about the use of grammar, vocabulary and punctuation in their own work. Chapters cover the following:

- Vocabulary
- Extending knowledge about grammar
- Punctuation
- Levels of formality
- Grammar for reading and writing
- Writing about language use
- Full glossary and further reading recommendations

Completely underpinned by the National Curriculum Programmes of Study for Key Stages 3 and 4, this book supports all secondary school English teachers, regardless of their chosen GCSE specification, and is essential reading for trainee, newly qualified and experienced teachers alike.

Geoff Barton is the General Secretary of the Association of School & College Leaders (ASCL). A former headteacher, he has also written and edited more than 100 books on English and school leadership. He is a Founding Fellow of the English Association and a regular writer and speaker on education.

Jo Shackleton has been a secondary English teacher and subject leader, consultant and inspector. She has been a curriculum adviser on the grammar, punctuation and spelling (GPS) test and is the author of *Grammar Survival for Primary Teachers*. She has provided training to teachers throughout the country on grammar and punctuation.

Grammar Survival for Secondary Teachers

A Practical Toolkit

Third edition

Geoff Barton and Jo Shackleton

Routledge
Taylor & Francis Group

LONDON AND NEW YORK

Third edition published 2019
by Routledge
2 Park Square, Milton Park, Abingdon, Oxon, OX14 4RN

and by Routledge
711 Third Avenue, New York, NY 10017

Routledge is an imprint of the Taylor & Francis Group, an informa business

© 2019 Geoff Barton and Jo Shackleton

The right of Geoff Barton and Jo Shackleton to be identified as authors
of this work has been asserted by them in accordance with sections 77
and 78 of the Copyright, Designs and Patents Act 1988.

All rights reserved. No part of this book may be reprinted or reproduced
or utilised in any form or by any electronic, mechanical, or other means,
now known or hereafter invented, including photocopying and recording,
or in any information storage or retrieval system, without permission in
writing from the publishers.

Trademark notice: Product or corporate names may be trademarks
or registered trademarks, and are used only for identification and
explanation without intent to infringe.

First edition published by Routledge 2006
Second edition published by Routledge 2010

British Library Cataloguing in Publication Data
A catalogue record for this book is available from the British Library

Library of Congress Cataloging in Publication Data
A catalog record has been requested for this book.

ISBN: 978-1-138-18524-1 (hbk)
ISBN: 978-1-138-18525-8 (pbk)
ISBN: 978-1-315-64460-8 (ebk)

Typeset in Minion
by Swales & Willis Ltd, Exeter, Devon, UK

Contents

Acknowledgements

Thanks to Dick Hudson and Margaret Fennell for their invaluable feedback during the drafting of this book.

Introduction

Much has changed in the world of secondary English since *Grammar Survival: A Teacher's Toolkit* was first published. We have a new national curriculum and new GCSEs with their challenging content, linear structure and different grading scale.

There have been huge changes at primary too: a quick glance at the key stage 2 curriculum shows how much grammar now has to be taught by the end of year 6, making sure that pupils are 'secondary ready', and raising the stakes in terms of what teachers need to know about grammar and punctuation.

For these reasons, we've significantly reworked this new edition of *Grammar Survival for Secondary Teachers*, bringing it up to date and making it current and relevant to secondary English teachers. It's completely underpinned by the national curriculum programmes of study for key stages 3 and 4, so you'll find it useful regardless of your chosen GCSE specification.

Like us, many of you are literature graduates, confident in the analysis of text and literary terminology, but perhaps less familiar with grammar and linguistic terminology. One teacher told us that she felt 'increasingly on the back foot with teaching grammar'. So this book is designed to support you, helping you to 'get on the front foot with grammar'.

Grammar Survival for Secondary Teachers aims to support your subject knowledge in an easy-to-use way. Each left-hand page sets out the knowledge you need about different aspects of grammar, incorporating research evidence where appropriate.

But it goes further, in that it aims to support pedagogy too. So each right-hand page deals with application, offering practical ideas and approaches for teaching grammar and punctuation, often in the context of appropriate and authentic texts so that your pupils can see grammar in action.

Grammar in the key stages 3 and 4 programmes of study might look a little thin compared to the amount of grammatical knowledge that must be taught at key stages 1 and 2. However, the task at secondary is vital – and hugely exciting – as it's about application. What's the point in knowing about grammar unless pupils can use that knowledge to become better readers and writers, speakers and listeners?

This book aims to help pupils become more confident and informed readers, able to make conscious choices as writers by drawing on the texts they read as models for their own independent writing.

There are five key emphases relating to grammar in the key stage 3 and 4 programmes of study which underpin the way we've approached this book:

1. Consolidating and building on the grammar taught at key stage 2

The test model at key stage 2 is a compensatory one, meaning that even pupils who've reached the expected standard may have gaps in their knowledge and understanding. You'll want to consolidate and build on your pupils' knowledge about grammar, making sure that their progress doesn't falter in the early years of key stage 3, and preparing them for the reading and writing demands of GCSE. You'll also need to identify any gaps in their knowledge and understanding which might become barriers to learning if left unaddressed.

2. **Extending pupils' knowledge about grammar and using it to analyse more challenging texts, focusing on effectiveness and impact**

There's detailed grammatical content in the primary curriculum, but very little in the secondary curriculum, where the focus is on application of that knowledge – analysing and evaluating, as a reader, the impact of a writer's choices of vocabulary, form, and grammatical and structural features. You'll want to build on the grammar taught at key stage 2, as well as introducing more challenging aspects of grammar, appropriate to key stages 3 and 4.

3. **Drawing on vocabulary and grammar in reading and listening, and consciously deploying these in writing and speech to achieve particular effects**

As writers, it's essential that we select appropriate vocabulary, grammatical structures, forms and organisational features that reflect the audience, purpose and context of our writing. We also know that reading informs writing: sharing a model and teasing out the writer's technique and choices and the way they impact on the reader; modelling short pieces of writing and thinking aloud as we write; deliberating on and orally rehearsing our choices; inviting pupils to share the composition with us, sifting and challenging their contributions – these fundamental approaches continue to underpin the teaching of writing and are key to the effective teaching of grammar.

4. **Understanding the differences between spoken and written language, formal and informal registers, Standard English and non-Standard varieties, and using Standard English in writing and speech**

Pupils are taught about Standard English and formal and informal registers at key stage 2. The challenge at secondary is to teach pupils to adapt language appropriately, according to audience and purpose, and in a wider range of more demanding contexts across the curriculum.

5. **Using linguistic and literary terminology precisely, accurately and confidently to discuss reading, writing, and spoken language**

There is some required grammatical terminology at key stage 2, and pupils are expected to use it when discussing their writing and reading. At secondary, literary and linguistic terminology combine to provide pupils with a metalanguage to critically evaluate language use.

So this newly revised book deals with all of this – and more. 'Text types' may well have disappeared from the curriculum, but there is – rightly – a huge emphasis on the need to adapt writing for a wide range of audiences and purposes, selecting the appropriate form by drawing on knowledge of vocabulary, grammar and text structure. Different types of text are explicitly referenced in the programmes of study, and represented in the various GCSE specifications. So we've included a whole chapter on grammar for reading and writing, exploring authentic and challenging texts written for different purposes and audiences, and analysing them in terms of their grammar – including structure and cohesion – to find out exactly how they create their impact.

There's a whole new chapter on vocabulary too, as we know how important this is in all subjects. Indeed, the increased emphasis on spelling, punctuation and grammar in geography, history and religious studies reinforces the need for a cross-curricular approach in schools.

We've retained a chapter on punctuation, as grammar and punctuation are so closely interrelated. We know that pupils benefit from seeing how the conventions of punctuation are linked to clarity and subtlety of meaning: being good at using punctuation makes us more effective writers.

There's also a glossary and further recommended reading at the end for those of you who'd like to take things further.

Above all, we really hope you find the book useful.

Jo Shackleton and Geoff Barton
March 2018

Chapter 1
Vocabulary

Words and their meanings

What you need to know about vocabulary

There's no denying the importance of vocabulary, whether it's finding the right words to express thoughts clearly and concisely in speech; reading and understanding more complex texts; or choosing words with precision in writing. When we 'know' a word, we not only know what it means, but also how to use it, and in what contexts. This is why, in the secondary curriculum, vocabulary sits alongside grammar, but is also threaded through the national curriculum programmes of study for reading, writing and spoken English.

As well as the expectation that pupils will develop a broad vocabulary for general use both in English and across the curriculum, there's also a requirement for pupils to use literary and linguistic vocabulary to discuss language. We'll look at this aspect of vocabulary in the final chapter.

While vocabulary size is strongly equated with success in reading, reading also provides an opportunity to acquire new words and identify other meanings of familiar words in new contexts. For pupils with a limited vocabulary, it's a vicious circle: reading can feel like an uphill struggle, making them less inclined to persevere and so reducing their opportunities to expand their vocabulary further.

Worryingly, research over many years has shown that pupils from low socio-economic groups typically start school with a smaller vocabulary than those from higher socio-economic groups – this is largely determined by parental practice, since children acquire larger vocabularies when they are exposed to rich oral language in the home. And as they grow older, the gap continues to widen: the more words we know, the more words we can generate. By the time pupils reach secondary age, the problem can be well advanced, with seemingly insurmountable differences between those who are word rich and those who are word poor – the so-called 'Matthew Effect'.

Good teaching can have a real impact though and – thanks to extensive research in this field – we now know what makes a difference in the classroom.

Research by Isabel L. Beck and colleagues highlights the importance of explicitly teaching the type of vocabulary that pupils need, but are unlikely to absorb through general exposure. They categorise vocabulary into three 'tiers', providing a useful reference point for teaching (Figure 1.1).

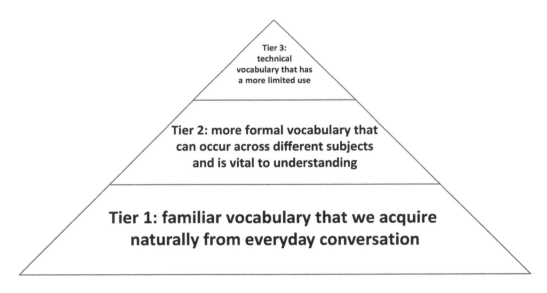

Figure 1.1 Tiers of vocabulary

Teaching about vocabulary

Over the past few years, most secondary schools have implemented various whole-school strategies to support pupils' vocabulary – but with varying degrees of success. For example, we might have found that our 'word of the week' – introduced in isolation – had little real impact. We might have encouraged pupils to use a thesaurus, only to find words inappropriately 'shoe-horned' into their writing as a result.

Steven A. Stahl provides an explanation for this. He tells us that 'knowing' a word involves more than just knowing the word's definition. It involves knowing how the word functions in different contexts – how it 'fits into the world' and how it relates to other words.

So we need to combine introduction of new vocabulary with multiple exposures to those words, alongside purposeful work on the way they function in different spoken and written contexts.

Teaching that promotes 'word consciousness' – where teachers and pupils regularly talk about words and their meanings, and where 'word play' is actively encouraged – is more likely to be successful in broadening pupils' vocabulary.

There's a range of research into the way children acquire a broad and rich vocabulary. While much of it relates to younger pupils, it applies to the secondary classroom too. Broadly speaking, the following approaches – when used in combination – are likely to be effective:

1. Drawing attention to new words and inciting interest, curiosity and pleasure in them
2. Encouraging reading (fiction and non-fiction) both at home and in school
3. Promoting high-quality talk, holding meaningful conversations, and modelling less familiar and more sophisticated vocabulary
4. Exposing pupils to new words on a number of occasions and in a variety of contexts, including multi-media methods
5. Making connections between words so that pupils can generate words, relating new words to words they already know (for example, drawing on word roots, prefixes and suffixes)
6. Teaching pupils strategies for working out the meaning of words they don't know (for example, by drawing on context, morphology or analogy)
7. Explicitly teaching pupils words that are essential to their understanding but which they are unlikely to meet through everyday exposure

We'll look at some of these approaches in more detail in the following pages. However, what's clear from this is that all teachers – not only teachers of English – must find a way to make sure that explicit teaching of vocabulary does happen. At the very least, this might involve having a list of key words in a lesson plan, plus key words to be reinforced from previous lessons.

What you need to know about more formal vocabulary

Much vocabulary is acquired naturally through everyday experiences, typically through spoken language in social situations. This is Beck and colleagues' 'tier 1' vocabulary, consisting of commonly used words that rarely need to be taught because pupils are already familiar with them. If pupils rely heavily on these words, however, their vocabulary may be limited; they may 'write as they speak' and find it difficult to adapt their speech and writing for more formal purposes and audiences.

By the time pupils arrive at secondary school, they need to be equipped to deal with the range of reading and writing they'll encounter across different subjects. They're likely to meet more formal vocabulary – the type of language that might appear in literary or academic texts. This is Beck et al.'s 'tier 2' vocabulary, and it's not necessarily the kind of vocabulary that tends to occur in everyday conversation. Pupils are less likely to be familiar with it unless they are confident, independent readers or regularly exposed to rich oral language at home.

Such words often have multiple meanings, depending on how they're used. They're words that allow us to express ourselves more precisely, or convey subtle nuances of meaning. They're words that pupils really need to know, as they're often key to their understanding as readers of more complex texts. As writers, familiarity with such words can be empowering too.

These words benefit from being explicitly taught. Unfortunately, because they're likely to appear frequently in subjects across the curriculum, it's not always clear whose responsibility it is to teach them.

Careful selection – and explicit teaching – of new words before pupils encounter them in a text, including multiple exposures to those words in meaningful and varied contexts, is strongly recommended. While this involves an element of preparation and pre-teaching, it's likely to pay dividends in the longer term. It's not unlike the approach we might take when introducing an older text like a play by Shakespeare.

When selecting 'tier 2' words for direct teaching, it's worth considering whether your pupils already understand the concepts the words describe, and whether you'll be able to explain them in a way they'll understand.

In the following passage, we may broadly agree on the words we might select for direct teaching, but there's no single correct response – it depends on your pupils and their prior knowledge. Which words are your pupils unlikely to know? Which words do they really need to know to fully understand the text?

Text A – using more formal 'tier 2' words	Text B – using less formal 'tier 1' words
As we approached the summit, a mist enveloped us and the tops of the mountains were suddenly shrouded with low cloud. Our supplies were rapidly diminishing, so it was essential to maintain morale . . .	As we got to the top, we were surrounded by mist, and low cloud covered the tops of the mountains. We didn't have much food left, so I knew I had to keep everybody's spirits up . . .

It's worth noting that Text B, more akin to spoken language, presents some difficulties of its own in the form of idiomatic language ('keep everybody's spirits up') which may not be familiar to all pupils.

Teaching about more formal vocabulary

One of the most helpful things you can do is to teach pupils how to make connections between words that are related by their meaning and structure. A focus on word origins and roots (etymology) and word structure (morphology) enables pupils to draw on their existing knowledge to generate more words – thus building vocabulary and supporting spelling.

Many English words have their roots in ancient Greek or Latin, and these roots carry meaning. For example, the root 'tract' (meaning 'drag' or 'pull') gives us tractor, distraction, protracted and intractable. The root 'dict' (meaning 'say') gives us edict, indictment, jurisdiction, dictator and contradict. You might give pupils a number of etymologically related words formed from the same root and ask them to work out their shared meaning. Alternatively, give them a root with its meaning such as 'bio' (life), 'rupt' (break, burst) or 'port' (carry) and ask them to find words formed from that root.

Similarly, a focus on root words (not the same as word roots) and affixes (prefixes and suffixes) can help pupils to generate words and spell them correctly (for example, depressed, pressing, impression, impressionable, impressive).

Explicit work on synonyms can lead to rich discussion about shades – or nuances – of related meaning implied by words that, on the surface, seem to mean the same thing. One way is to give pupils a set of synonyms on cards and ask them to arrange them on a continuum – the least formal to the most formal. You can ask pupils to discuss the connotations of each word. This is best done collaboratively, in pairs or small groups, as it's likely to promote rich discussion as well as some healthy debate. There are two examples below to get you started, but you can use a good thesaurus to add to the list.

buy	purchase	pay for	procure	acquire	invest in	snap up	secure

talk	chat	converse	discourse	utter	speak	parley	confer

→ verbs taking adverb particles/prepositional particles.

Preposition and phrasal verbs are also worth exploring, and pupils can be encouraged to suggest their more formal equivalents.

← presses relationship

approve of = condone	work out = calculate	look at = regard	come up with = devise	look forward to = anticipate

Active reading approaches such as text completion (cloze) can help to draw attention not only to connotation, but also to precision of word choice. It's probably best to choose a short extract from a text the class is studying. What's more, discussion of the relative merits of each word can also support pupils' own editing skills. Here's a passage from *Great Expectations*, where Pip encounters Miss Havisham.

From that room, too, the daylight was completely _____1_____ , and it had an airless smell that was _____2_____. A fire had been lately _____3_____ in the damp old-fashioned grate, and it was more _____4_____ to go out than to burn up, and the _____5_____ smoke which hung in the room seemed colder than the clearer air – like our own marsh mist.

1. excluded, barred, eliminated
2. oppressive, stuffy, uncomfortable
3. kindled, lit, ignited
4. disposed, minded, likely
5. reluctant, bashful, apprehensive

What you need to know about subject-specific vocabulary

Some vocabulary, consisting of more technical, subject-specific words, is best taught as the need arises within the relevant subject. Because these words tend to be specific to a particular field of study, they're encountered less frequently and have limited general use outside of that field. However, within their subject area, they can be key to understanding a particular concept. This is Beck et al.'s 'tier 3' vocabulary.

Here are some examples:

English Literature	Geography	Science	Mathematics
• Oxymoron • Stanza • Iambic pentameter • Allegorical • Pathetic fallacy	• Glaciation • Hydrology • Topography • Eco system • Tectonic plate	• Micro-organism • Chrysalis • Molecule • Enzyme • Photosynthesis	• Hypotenuse • Equilateral • Trigonometry • Equation • Algebraic

Subject-specific vocabulary is associated with register. This is the term that refers to the specific language (typically vocabulary) used by particular groups or professions when talking or writing about their own field of interest and expertise. Legalese, for example, is the specialised language used by lawyers that most of us without a legal background may struggle to comprehend. You'll be able to think of others: teachers, for example, use particular words and expressions when talking about pedagogy and the curriculum which others may not be familiar with.

One important feature of register is the way some words can take on different meanings when they're used in a subject-specific way. They may well be part of the common register, but they might also have a different meaning in a particular subject. Pupils may be familiar with a word's common register use, but they'll need explicit teaching about its meaning in more specific contexts.

Word	Common register meaning	Subject-specific meaning
Conceit	Excessive pride in oneself	In English literature, an ingenious or witty thought or image
Plates	Flat dishes, typically used to serve food	In geography, rigid slabs made of the Earth's crust that move relative to one another
Cell	A small room in which a prisoner is locked up	In biology, the smallest structural and functional unit of an organism
Gravity	Extreme importance or seriousness	In physics, the force that attracts objects towards each other (in particular, the force that makes things fall to the ground)

Teaching about subject-specific vocabulary

Researchers tend to agree that it's helpful for pupils to have an understanding of a concept before introducing the terminology that defines it. They also agree that simply providing definitions for pupils to copy or stick in their books is less helpful than actively involving pupils in constructing their own definitions. A UK study in 2007 found that, although students made gains when explanations were provided for unfamiliar words, they made the greatest increases when they explained their own definitions of the targeted words.

Once you've taught terminology, you can check and reinforce it through the use of activities such as the 'word loop' game. This involves giving each pupil a card with a definition on the left-hand side and a word (that doesn't match the definition) on the right. This is a quick-fire activity that can be done at the beginning or end of a lesson. One pupil starts the 'loop' by reading out their word. The pupil who has the matching definition reads it out, then reads their word and so on until the loop is complete.

Here's an example of some 'word loop' cards based on literary terminology:

A comparison between two things using the words 'like' or 'as'	Metaphor
A way of comparing two things by stating that one thing is another	Empathy
A feeling of identification with a character	Irony
A form of sarcasm involving two layers of meaning: a surface meaning and the real meaning beneath the surface	Protagonist
The main character in a novel, film or play	Simile

Some subject-specific words lend themselves to the etymological approaches on the previous pages. For example, much scientific and mathematical vocabulary has a Greek or Latin root linked to its meaning from which pupils can generalise. Here are some examples:

- Equilateral (equi = equal)
- Trigonometry (tri = three)
- Thermometer (therm = heat)
- Microscope (micro = small)

In geography, the meaning of words like hydrology and topography can be inferred through knowledge of roots and meanings. Pupils might be asked to think of other words formed from particular roots, or using particular affixes.

In English lessons, we can make the connection between words like pathos, empathy, sympathy and antipathy – all formed from the word root 'path' meaning 'feeling'. (Just be aware that 'path' can also mean 'disease' so it's important not to confuse words with this meaning.)

What you need to know about troublesome words

Some words are commonly confused, even by the most fluent language users. Many of these are homophones (words that have the same pronunciation but different meanings and spellings). The following words (most of which are homophones) are often confused.

AFFECT OR EFFECT?

- Affect is a verb, meaning to have an effect on (Bob was badly affected by the experience).
- Effect is a noun, meaning a result or consequence (The film had a huge effect on Bob).

Note that 'effect' can also be a verb, meaning to bring something about or make it happen (The last government effected big changes in social policy).

BOUGHT OR BROUGHT?

- Bought is the simple past form and –ed participle of the verb to buy (She bought a caravan with her savings).
- Brought is the simple past form and –ed participle of the verb to bring (She brought her dog into the office every day).

COMPLEMENT OR COMPLIMENT?

- Complement can be a noun or a verb, meaning improvement or completion:
  o We have a full complement of teachers this year.
  o That parsley sauce really complemented the fish.
- Compliment can also be a noun or a verb, but it means praise or admiration:
  o Jonny paid his team a huge compliment when he praised their achievements.
  o Jonny complimented his team on their hard work.

DISCREET OR DISCRETE?

- Discreet is an adjective, meaning unobtrusive or tactful (Their landlady was very discreet when dealing with enquiries from the press).
- Discrete is also an adjective, but it means distinct or separate (Physics, biology and chemistry are taught as discrete subjects).

PASSED OR PAST?

- Passed is the simple past form and –ed participle of the verb to pass:
  o We passed the new shopping centre on our way to the airport
  o Have you passed your driving test?
- Past can be a noun (We always did it like this in the past), an adjective (The past few days have been difficult), a preposition (We drove past the building site) or an adverb (A week went past and we heard nothing), but never a verb.

PRINCIPAL OR PRINCIPLE?

- Principal can be an adjective or a noun, meaning the first, main or most important thing:
  o My principal concern is that the new road will destroy ancient woodland.
  o Our new college principal starts next term.
- Principle is a noun, meaning an idea, rule or belief (I have strong principles and I won't buy products that have been tested on animals).

Teaching about troublesome words

Most of these words will have been taught in key stage 2 so, if they're still proving difficult by the time pupils reach secondary school, they're likely to need some attention.

Visual prompts, prominently displayed in the classroom, can provide helpful reminders for words such as lightening/lightning, currant/current or desert/dessert. Better still, get pupils to make their own.

It makes sense to have a handful of good dictionaries and thesauruses available in every classroom, but make sure that pupils know where they are and how to use them. Model their use yourself so that pupils see you using them too. If pupils are using online dictionaries, make sure they know how to choose a reputable source.

Self-help strategies and aide memoirs are vital when there's no other way of checking a word. For example, with tricky words like 'advise/advice', 'devise/device', 'license/licence', and 'practise/practice', remind pupils that the 's' spelling is used for the verb and the 'c' spelling for the noun. It will help if they learn just one pair of words (like 'advise/advice' or 'devise/device'), where the difference in pronunciation is clear.

If you've been focusing attention on roots and affixes, a word like 'autobiography' can be broken into its component parts to reveal its meaning (auto = self, bio = life, graph = writing).

In reading, it's sometimes possible to use contextual clues to infer the meaning of unfamiliar words. You can show pupils how to look for examples, elaboration, synonyms, antonyms, or even noun phrases in apposition (see the next chapter). It can be reassuring to know that sometimes – even if you don't instantly know a word – you might be able to find its meaning by looking for clues in the rest of the sentence. For example:

- Many <u>crustaceans</u>, such as crabs, lobsters and crayfish, live in the sea. (Look for examples.)
- When researching on the Internet, it's important to check that you're using a <u>reputable</u> source – one you can trust that isn't likely to contain errors or misleading information. (Look for elaboration.)
- Some people are <u>adept</u> at helping others; they are skilful at spotting when others need assistance. (Look for a synonym.)
- The <u>disconsolate</u> child would not stop weeping: his misery was plain for all to see. (Look for synonymous meaning.)
- My last teacher was such a <u>disciplinarian</u>. Whereas other teachers were easy-going, she put us in detention at lunchtime for the slightest misdemeanors. (Look for an antonym.)
- His <u>missive</u>, another one of his long letters, arrived by post yesterday. (Look for a noun phrase in apposition.)

Chapter 2
Extending knowledge about grammar

Extending knowledge about grammar

What you need to know about extending knowledge about grammar

There's a lot of grammar in the primary national curriculum. Pupils are taught about the eight main word classes: nouns, verbs, adjectives, adverbs, pronouns, prepositions, determiners and conjunctions. They're taught about different types of phrases (such as noun phrases and preposition phrases) as well as clauses, including co-ordinated, subordinate and relative clauses. They learn about the passive voice and Standard English, as well as formal and informal vocabulary and grammatical structures. They learn about tense, cohesion and even the subjunctive mood!

You might be forgiven for thinking there's not much left for you to teach at key stages 3 and 4, especially since there's very little detail in the programmes of study.

Of course you'll want to build on and extend your pupils' knowledge about grammar and use it to analyse the texts they're studying at key stages 3 and 4. And you'll want them to apply their knowledge about grammar to their own writing too.

But initially, you'll want to address any gaps in their knowledge, taking care to avoid unnecessary repetition of learning that's already been secured.

National curriculum tests at the end of key stage 2 use a compensatory (rather than mastery) model so even pupils who achieve a high score could still potentially have gaps in their knowledge and understanding.

So you'll need to check what they already know and understand. It might be tempting just to give them another test, but far better to use your existing formative assessment methods to check their understanding in the context of their year 7 work.

It's important to find out what they already know without overly exposing pupils; after all, you want them to be curious about grammar – not wary of it! So try a 'little and often' approach and keep it interactive and engaging.

We've already seen in the previous chapter how teaching that promotes 'word consciousness' – where teachers and pupils regularly talk about words and their meanings, and where 'word play' is actively encouraged – is more likely to be successful in broadening pupils' vocabulary. There's no reason why this shouldn't apply to language more broadly.

You might give pupils a series of thought-provoking 'mini-challenges'. For example, ask them to work in pairs to compose sentences that use a given word in different ways. For example:

- Compose a sentence that uses 'bank' as a noun.
- Compose a sentence that uses 'bank' as a verb.
- Compose a sentence that uses 'creaking' twice – as a verb and as an adjective.
- Compose a sentence that uses 'after' as a subordinating conjunction.
- Compose a sentence that uses 'after' as a preposition.

Or you could play 'clause consequences'. Write a sentence on the board (it must contain at least one subordinate clause; for example, *As I scanned the hillside, I spied a puff of smoke*). Then ask pupils to choose from a set of cards, each containing an instruction. For example:

- Change the subject of the sentence
- Change the verb in the subordinate clause
- Embed the subordinate clause within the main clause
- Add a relative clause

You can ask pupils to compose and share orally, or they could write on mini whiteboards.

Alternatively, you could give pupils a set of 'composition cards' and ask them to follow the instructions to compose sentences. If you want to check their understanding even further, you could give them the instructions without the accompanying examples. Or you could ask them to match the instructions to the examples.

Instruction	Example
Compose a sentence which begins with a fronted subordinate clause.	Since the weather is so bad, the match will be cancelled.
Compose a sentence which begins with a preposition phrase.	During the night, we heard the thunder and saw the lightning.
Compose a single-clause sentence.	Tommy glanced out of his bedroom window.
Compose a sentence that has an expanded noun phrase as its subject.	A team of scientists in South America has just discovered a rare species of plant.
Compose a sentence with three independent clauses joined by different co-ordinating conjunctions.	Margo is a keen cyclist and she swims regularly, but she's never enjoyed team sports.
Compose a sentence that contains a relative clause.	The tourists whose luggage was destroyed by the fire have been awarded compensation.

Another way is to use an investigative approach, which requires pupils to draw on their existing knowledge to surface and seal new learning. Investigative approaches work best when there is one clear rule which pupils can articulate so they can generalise from the examples. Give pupils some sentences that (correctly) use the rule or convention you want to explore (you'll need enough examples – at least 10–12 – for the rule to be apparent) and ask them to articulate a simple explanation. You'll find an example of a comma investigation in the next chapter.

A 'creative imitation' approach, which enables pupils to borrow from reading and learn from more experienced writers, can be really powerful: this is an apprentice model, whereby young writers internalise the patterns of language, trying them on for size, before adapting and importing them into their own writing. It can be used with longer pieces of text or with a single sentence. For example, you could unpick the sentence below and then ask pupils to borrow the grammar and punctuation to write a sentence of their own. We'll return to this approach later in the book.

As she glanced around the room, her gaze settled on the scruffy-looking boy in the corner: from that moment, Sam's fate was sealed.

What you need to know about verb forms and tense

Verbs can take different forms and can be used in the present or the past tense:

- The simple form (She sings/sang in a band).
- The progressive (or continuous) form (I am/was playing in the football tournament).
- The present perfect (We have walked for miles and are exhausted).
- The past perfect (They had walked for miles before they saw the sign).

It's also possible to combine the progressive and perfect forms (It has/had been raining all week).

Many grammarians refer to the progressive and perfect forms as 'aspects' since they indicate the time frame of an action or event – for example, whether it is completely finished, still in progress, or complete but still relevant to the present time.

The historic present tense is generally accepted as the use of the present tense to describe past events, typically in narratives (true or fictional) and usually in speech or more informal writing. It can create a sense of immediacy:

- So she walks into the shop and she pauses at the door and then she says . . .

FINITE AND NON-FINITE VERBS

A finite verb is a verb that has a subject and shows its tense (The cheetah leapt into the air).

In contrast, a non-finite verb doesn't reveal its tense and is sometimes referred to as a non-tensed verb. Non-finite verbs are formed in one of three ways.

1. The –ed form (sometimes called the past participle or the –ed participle):

   Cheered by the crowd, the athletes raced towards the finishing line.

2. The –ing form (sometimes called the present participle or the –ing participle):

   He hurried to the bus stop, limping slightly.

3. The infinitive form (the base form of the verb preceded by 'to'):

   To swim the English Channel, she trained every day for a year.

Non-finite verbs introduce non-finite clauses and we'll look at these later in this chapter.

MODAL VERBS

Modality relates to the way we express attitudes such as possibility, probability, certainty, necessity and ability. This is largely achieved through modal verbs, but some adverbs and their related nouns and adjectives can do this too (probably, in all probability, it is probable that . . .).

There are nine core modal verbs: can, could, may, might, must, shall, should, will and would. Some grammarians also recognise ought to and used to as semi-modals (or marginal modals).

The meanings conveyed by modal verbs can be quite subtle.

- They express shades of meaning related to possibility, probability and certainty. (I might tidy my room in a moment. I will tidy my room in a moment.)
- They carry meaning related to permission, obligation and compulsion. (May I tidy my room now? I really should tidy my room now. I must tidy my room now.)
- They allow us to refer to future time. (I shall never forget you. I'll treasure these memories forever.)
- And they can convey politeness and an element of formality. (Would you pass the sauce? Might I have a word?)

Teaching about verb forms and tense

Pupils are taught quite a lot about verbs at key stages 1 and 2. They're taught about different verb forms, including the simple form, the progressive form and the perfect forms. They're taught about modal verbs, as well as the imperative and subjunctive moods. They're also taught how to use different suffixes, such as –ate, –ise and –ify to form verbs from other word classes.

There are several ways to consolidate and build on this knowledge at key stages 3 and 4.

One way is to explore the way modals can convey a range of subtle meanings such as tentativeness and guarded opinion. For example, in the following extract from a formal argument against school uniform, you can see how the modals (might/may/may) initially convey an element of uncertainty in order to acknowledge the counter argument which is later dismissed by the more certain 'won't' (will not). In the second example, an extract from a letter to parents about a school ski trip, the modals (may/will/will) enable the writer to acknowledge parents' potential concerns while providing reassurance to allay their fears.

> Some <u>might</u> say that school uniform prepares pupils for employment. They say that pupils <u>may</u> need to dress smartly in a work environment. They <u>may</u> even join a profession which requires a uniform to be worn, such as the police force or an airline. But this <u>won't</u> be the case for the majority of pupils. How many girls are actually likely to wear a tie once they leave school?

> As parents, you <u>may</u> be concerned about your child's safety on the ski slopes, but they <u>will</u> be taught by experienced and qualified instructors who <u>will</u> place your child's welfare at the heart of everything they do.

Another way is to pay attention to the conscious choice and control of verb forms and tense within writing. Tense consistency doesn't necessarily mean using the same tense all the way through a piece of writing: it's about choosing the appropriate verb forms to indicate the time frame of events or actions depicted in our writing. So, in the following extracts, it's perfectly appropriate to move from the past to the present and vice versa:

> The team's star player <u>scored</u> two goals at yesterday's match. A keen footballer since childhood, she <u>has been training</u> hard and <u>is</u> now one of our best young centre-forwards.

> I <u>write</u> to complain about your crunchy oat cereal which I <u>bought</u> from my local supermarket last week. I <u>have been enjoying</u> this cereal for several years, but you seem to <u>have changed</u> one of the main ingredients, which <u>means</u> that I <u>am</u> now unable to eat it.

Similarly, you might discuss the way writers use tense to create time shifts or flashbacks in novels.

Sometimes, pupils do tend to switch inappropriately from past to present (or vice versa) in their writing, especially if they get carried away with a strong narrative thread in a story, or don't pay attention to re-reading and editing their work. If this is the case with your pupils, it's worth exploring it explicitly, perhaps by displaying a piece of writing on a visualiser and modelling how to edit for tense consistency. Reinforce this regularly, and make it a clear expectation that pupils will edit and proof read their work as part of the writing process.

What you need to know about nouns and noun phrases

1. Nominalisation means forming a noun from another word class – usually a verb or an adjective. You can see how this works in the following sentences:

Without nominalisation	With nominalisation
The governors were dismayed when the headteacher disappeared.	The <u>disappearance</u> of the headteacher caused much <u>dismay</u>.
The hurricane swept through the islands, killing many people and destroying their homes.	The hurricane swept through the islands, causing <u>death</u> and <u>destruction</u>.

2. A gerund is an –ing form of a verb that functions as a noun:

   - <u>Swimming</u> is a great activity if you want to keep fit.
   - <u>Eating</u> is not allowed in the library.
   - The quality of <u>teaching</u> is much improved.

3. A noun phrase is a group of words with a noun or pronoun as its 'head' (although some grammarians accept a single noun or pronoun as a noun phrase). Here are some examples:

a freshly dug <u>molehill</u>	The head noun (molehill) is pre-modified by a determiner (a), an adverb (freshly) and an adjective formed from an –ed verb form or past participle (dug).
that rusty old car with two flat tyres	The head noun (car) is pre-modified by a determiner (that), two adjectives (rusty and old) and post-modified by a preposition phrase (with two flat tyres).
my eccentric uncle who lives on a boat in the Scottish Highlands	As well as being pre-modified, the head noun (uncle) is post-modified by a relative clause incorporating two preposition phrases.
that rusty old car with two flat tyres dumped on a side street near the canal	As well as being pre-modified, the head noun (car) is post-modified by a preposition phrase and a non-finite relative clause incorporating two further preposition phrases.

4. Noun phrases in apposition (two noun phrases positioned next to each other that refer to the same thing) can also constitute a single noun phrase since one modifies the other. The second noun phrase gives more information about the first.

   - <u>My neighbour</u>, <u>a friendly woman called Gladys</u>, has lived next door to us for thirty years.
   - <u>Mr Thomas</u>, <u>our new teacher</u>, is organising the geography field trip this year.

5. A nominal (or noun) clause is a clause that functions as a noun or noun phrase. Like a noun or noun phrase, it can be the subject of a sentence.

   - <u>What I really wanted</u> was a nice cup of tea.
   - <u>That he had been lying to me for over a year</u> suddenly became very clear.
   - <u>Learning to swim</u> takes a lot of perseverance.

Teaching about nouns and noun phrases

Pupils are taught about nouns and noun phrases at key stages 1 and 2. They're also taught how to use different suffixes, such as –er, –ness, –ment and –ation to form nouns from other word classes.

There are several ways to build on this knowledge at key stages 3 and 4.

NOMINALISATION

This is a particularly good way of helping pupils to write in a crisper, more succinct style. It tends to create 'noun-heavy' text which can feel quite weighty, but the effect is often one of greater concision, formality and objectivity.

You might ask pupils to compare the following two sentences:

- The club manager has resigned only two months after he was appointed: this has led many to wonder why he has left so soon.
- The <u>resignation</u> of the club manager so soon after his <u>appointment</u> has caused much <u>speculation</u>, as the <u>reasons</u> for his <u>departure</u> are unclear.

EXPANDING NOUN PHRASES USING RELATIVE AND NON-FINITE CLAUSES

Nouns carry the weight of meaning in sentences. If your pupils' writing would benefit from greater detail, this can often be done more efficiently by expanding the noun phrase rather than writing additional sentences.

At key stage 2, pupils might learn to expand noun phrases using determiners, adjectives, adverbs, other nouns or a preposition phrase. However, too much pre-modification can feel unwieldy (for example, <u>the creepy, dilapidated, haunted, old house</u>) so this is where post-modification can be useful.

At key stage 3, you might go further with post-modification, using relative and non-finite clauses. For example:

- Two hedgehogs <u>that we found curled up in the compost heap at the bottom of our garden</u> (the head noun 'hedgehogs' is post-modified by a relative clause)
- A tantalising glimpse of the sun <u>slipping down below the horizon</u> (the post-modification of the head noun 'glimpse' includes a non-finite clause)

Expanded noun phrases enable us to compress a large amount of detail into a limited number of words, often with the effect of greater concision and precision. Ask pupils to look at some cookery books or restaurant menus to see how different dishes are described using expanded noun phrases:

> Topside of beef braised in a red wine reduction
>
> Fillet of sea bream served on a bed of sweet potato mash
>
> Homemade quiche accompanied by mixed salad leaves tossed in a balsamic dressing

Or you could explore travel writing or promotional literature where detailed description is achieved through an abundance of expanded noun phrases:

> We set sail for the Greek islands: a coastline of sandy beaches and hidden coves shimmering in the Aegean sun; a glimpse of an ancient ruin nestled on the horizon; white-washed, blue-domed churches.

What you need to know about relative clauses

A relative clause is a type of subordinate clause that post-modifies a noun to create an expanded noun phrase. It is typically introduced by a relative pronoun (who, whom, whose, which, that), although the relative adverbs (when, where, why) can also be used.

- This is the book <u>that I want</u>.
- The train, <u>which was already full</u>, pulled into the station.
- Is there anybody <u>who can help me</u>?
- That was the moment <u>when I realised he was lying</u>.
- This is the place <u>where I want to live</u>.
- The reason <u>why she left</u> is a mystery to me.

(Remember that <u>where</u>, <u>when</u> and <u>that</u> can also function as subordinating conjunctions to introduce a straightforward subordinate clause so be careful not to confuse these with relative clauses.)

Sometimes the relative pronoun is omitted altogether: this is also referred to as a 'zero' or 'implied' relative pronoun.

- This is the book <u>I want</u>.
- That was the moment <u>I realised he was lying</u>.

Relative clauses can be defining (restrictive) or non-defining (non-restrictive).

Defining relative clauses define the noun they follow:

- My friend <u>who lives in London</u> is selling her house.

The relative clause (who lives in London) refers to my specific friend who lives in London rather than any of my other friends who live elsewhere.

Non-defining relative clauses provide additional information that is not essential to the meaning.

- My friend, <u>who lives in London</u>, is selling her house.

The fact that my friend lives in London is interesting, but non-essential, information.

There are two things that you need to know about non-defining relative clauses:

- A pair of commas, brackets or dashes is used to buffer it from the main clause, as it provides information that could be removed from the sentence without changing its meaning.
- The relative pronoun 'that' tends <u>not</u> to be used to introduce a non-defining relative clause.

Sentential relative clauses refer back to a preceding clause or sentence and are introduced by the relative pronoun 'which'.

- She decided to train to be a hairdresser, <u>which was a really good idea</u>.
- After we'd visited Australia, we travelled on to New Zealand – <u>which meant we were away for a month longer than planned</u>.

Teaching about relative clauses

Pupils are taught about relative clauses introduced by <u>who</u>, <u>which</u>, <u>where</u>, <u>when</u>, <u>whose</u>, <u>that</u> or a 'zero' relative pronoun at key stage 2.

One of the growth points at secondary is to teach pupils how to use a relative clause to post-modify a noun in an expanded noun phrase:

- The hotel <u>that used to be on the seafront</u> . . .
- The hotel <u>whose owners are moving to Spain</u> . . .
- The hotel <u>which was recently refurbished at great expense</u> . . .

Furthermore, pupils are unlikely to know about defining and non-defining relative clauses, so this is also territory worth exploring at key stage 3. It's not that they particularly need to know the terminology (although it's useful for them to have the language to discuss their writing) but there are clear implications for both punctuation and meaning.

Compare the difference in meaning between the following two sentences:

1. The customers, who queued all night outside the shop, got some great bargains in the sale.
2. The customers who queued all night outside the shop got some great bargains in the sale.

The difference in meaning is subtle but clear. In the first sentence, all of the customers got some great bargains; in the second sentence, only those customers who queued all night got the bargains. By implication, those who turned up later did not. It's the commas that signal this important semantic difference, as they buffer the non-defining clause from the main clause, meaning that it could be removed without affecting the meaning.

If you're teaching pupils to write in a very formal style, it's helpful for them to know about the relative pronoun 'whom'. This tends to be used in very formal writing, although it's always used following a preposition.

- I attended the farewell gathering for my old headteacher, <u>for whom</u> I had the utmost respect.
- We were sorry to quarrel with our neighbours, <u>with whom</u> we had always enjoyed a very good relationship.
- I am indebted to Laura, my only daughter, <u>to whom</u> I leave my entire estate . . .

However, it's quite acceptable, especially in speech and more informal writing, to separate the preposition from its pronoun.

- I attended the farewell gathering for my old headteacher, <u>who</u> I had the utmost respect <u>for</u>.
- We were sorry to quarrel with our neighbours, <u>who</u> we had always enjoyed a very good relationship <u>with</u>.
- I am indebted to Laura, my only daughter, <u>who</u> I leave my entire estate <u>to</u> . . .

This can sound a little clunky in very formal writing, so it's good for pupils to have the choice.

What you need to know about non-finite clauses

A non-finite clause is a type of subordinate clause introduced by a non-finite verb. Because non-finite clauses don't indicate tense, the reader has to look to the main clause to find the subject and the tense of the verb.

Here are some examples:

A non-finite clause using the –ed form	<u>Supported by her friends and family</u>, Alice went on to train for a place in the Olympics.
A non-finite clause using the –ing form	<u>Whimpering softly</u>, the boy was on the point of giving up when he saw a dim light in the distance.
A non-finite clause using the infinitive form	The athlete had trained every day <u>to win her gold medal</u>.

Non-finite clauses are highly mobile and can be moved to different positions in a sentence for effect and emphasis.

- <u>Sobbing loudly</u>, the small child picked up his bicycle.
- The small child, <u>sobbing loudly</u>, picked up his bicycle.
- The small child picked up his bicycle, <u>sobbing loudly</u>.

Non-finite clauses can function as relative clauses. However, they can be difficult to spot because the relative pronoun is omitted.

Finite relative clause	Non-finite relative clause
The boy <u>who was standing at the window</u> seemed to wave at us, but then he vanished.	The boy <u>standing at the window</u> seemed to wave at us, but then he vanished.
The errors <u>that are marked in red</u> need to be corrected.	The errors <u>marked in red</u> need to be corrected.
The hotel, <u>which is nestled in the bay overlooking the sea</u>, is very popular with tourists.	The hotel, <u>nestled in the bay overlooking the sea</u>, is very popular with tourists.

Teaching about non-finite clauses

Pupils are unlikely to be taught about non-finite clauses at key stage 2, although they may well be familiar with –ing verbs and –ed verbs and the way they can be used in different positions in a sentence.

- <u>Hissing softly</u>, the adder slithered through the long grass.
- Freddie, <u>smirking slyly</u>, glanced behind him.
- The athletes passed the finishing line, <u>cheered on by the crowd</u>.
- <u>Drenched by the rain</u>, I sheltered in the doorway.

Use of non-finite clauses can really help pupils to expand and vary their sentence structure so this is an important aspect of grammar to develop in key stage 3.

One of the most helpful things to teach is their mobility within the sentence. You might explore the shifts in emphasis and meaning created by the positioning of the non-finite clause, teasing out, through discussion, the impact on the reader. For example, a fronted clause is foregrounded and therefore given more emphasis. However, by placing it after the main clause, its impact is delayed and potentially heightened. It's good for pupils to have these choices.

- <u>Coughing breathlessly</u>, the old vagrant shuffled along the road.
- The old vagrant, <u>coughing breathlessly</u>, shuffled along the road.
- The old vagrant shuffled along the road, <u>coughing breathlessly</u>.

- <u>Dismayed by the sudden turn of events</u>, Jim decided to hand in his notice.
- Jim, <u>dismayed by the sudden turn of events</u>, decided to hand in his notice.
- Jim decided to hand in his notice, <u>dismayed by the sudden turn of events</u>.

Or you might explore their use in literature. In this extract from *Bleak House*, Dickens' use of non-finite relative causes (underlined) is remarkable. The non-finite –ing verbs create a sense of relentless continuity, contributing to the atmosphere of inexorability, misery and oppression.

> Fog everywhere. Fog up the river, where it flows among the green aits and meadows; fog down the river, where it rolls defiled among the tiers of shipping, and the waterside pollution of a great (and dirty) city. Fog on the Essex marshes; fog on the Kentish heights. Fog <u>creeping into the cabooses of collier brigs</u>; fog <u>lying out on the yards</u>, and <u>hovering in the rigging of great ships</u>; fog <u>drooping on the gunwales of barges and small boats</u>. Fog in the eyes and throats of ancient Greenwich pensioners, <u>wheezing by the firesides of their wards</u>; fog in the stem and bowl of the afternoon pipe of the wrathful skipper, down in his close cabin; fog <u>cruelly pinching the fingers and toes of his shivering little 'prentice' boy on deck</u>. Chance people on the bridges <u>peeping over the parapets into a nether sky of fog</u>, with fog all around them, as if they were up in a balloon, and <u>hanging in the misty clouds</u>.

Extending knowledge about grammar

What you need to know about conditionals

Conditionals deal with hypothetical situations and their consequences. A conditional clause is typically introduced by the subordinating conjunction 'if', although other subordinators can be used, such as <u>when</u>, <u>unless</u>, or <u>on condition that</u>.

    The conditional clause is typically fronted, but it may follow the main clause.

Some conditionals express truths that are constant or general.

- I feel good <u>if I exercise regularly</u>.
- <u>When the clocks go back</u>, it gets dark earlier.
- Our roof leaks <u>when it rains heavily</u>.
- <u>If there's a high tide</u>, our beach hut floods.

Some conditionals express 'real' situations that haven't yet happened, but are likely or possible.

- <u>If I finish this work by lunchtime</u>, I'll go swimming.
- You can't go to Jane's party <u>unless you apologise</u>.

Some conditionals express 'unreal' situations: they deal with things that are hypothetical, unlikely or even impossible.

- <u>If I'd bought a lottery ticket</u>, I might have been a millionaire by now.
- <u>If I'd known you were feeling ill</u>, I wouldn't have dreamt of asking you to babysit.

In more formal writing, conditionals are sometimes used with the subjunctive 'were' form.

- <u>If I were in your position</u>, I would apologise immediately.
- <u>If it were possible to change the date</u>, it would be more convenient.

Very formal conditionals reverse the word order and omit the conjunction. This type of conditional clause starts with 'had', 'should' or the subjunctive 'were'.

- <u>Had we known about this in advance</u>, we would never have agreed.
- <u>Should you experience any further problems</u>, please contact us immediately.
- <u>Were I to investigate this further</u>, I may well uncover some rather unpleasant truths.

Teaching about conditionals

Like the subjunctive, conditionals deal with hypothetical situations. However, while the subjunctive does feature in the primary curriculum, conditionals don't, so it's unlikely that pupils will have any explicit knowledge of them. Since we use conditionals commonly in everyday conversation, more explicit knowledge should help pupils express more abstract ideas with greater precision.

Conditionals can be useful in speech or writing that requires an element of concession, supposition or qualification (for example, when writing a balanced argument or holding a formal debate).

Discussion topic	Conditional clauses
What would be in your election manifesto if you were prime minister?	• <u>If I had the power to make major decisions affecting the country</u>, I would start by . . . • <u>Should I be fortunate enough to be elected</u>, I would . . .
Some people spend a lot of money on expensive adventures, like round-the-world trips. Is this a good use of their time and money?	• <u>Unless people experience the urge to travel</u>, they may never . . . • <u>If people choose to spend their money on luxury travel</u>, they shouldn't . . .
Have mobile phones been the greatest invention of the twentieth century, or are they the scourge of our time?	• <u>Had mobile phones never been invented</u>, we might . . . • <u>If we'd never had mobile phones</u>, we'd still be . . .

Alternatively, you might give pupils some hypothetical situations based on a literature text you're studying and ask them to work them through to their conclusion:

• If Macbeth hadn't encountered the witches . . .
• If Antonio had refused to help Bassanio . . .
• If Miranda had been a boy . . .
• If Tybalt had only injured Mercutio . . .

What you need to know about the passive voice

We have a choice of two 'voices' – active or passive – and this choice affects the way we present information in a clause. The active voice is far more frequently used in both speech and writing, whereas the passive voice is less common.

In the active voice, the subject is also the 'agent' – in other words, the one that carries out the action expressed by the verb:

<u>Surgeons</u> performed a ground-breaking operation yesterday to restore a man's eyesight.

In the passive voice, the subject is not the agent – rather, it's the recipient of the action expressed by the verb – or the one that's affected by it. A preposition phrase (usually headed up by the preposition 'by') indicates the agent, but its use is optional.

<u>A ground-breaking operation</u> was performed (by surgeons) yesterday to restore a man's eyesight.

Changing from active to passive:

1. The subject in the active clause (surgeons) moves to the end in the passive clause. Although it continues to be the agent, it is no longer the subject of the clause. It is introduced by the preposition 'by'.

   <u>Surgeons</u> performed a ground-breaking operation . . .

   A ground-breaking operation was performed by <u>surgeons</u> . . .

2. The object of the active clause (a ground-breaking operation) moves to the front in the passive clause, where it becomes the subject.

   Surgeons performed <u>a ground-breaking operation</u> . . .

   <u>A ground-breaking operation</u> was performed by surgeons . . .

3. The verb 'to be' is put into the same tense as the verb in the active clause (performed). The past (–ed) participle of the verb in the active clause is used.

   Surgeons <u>performed</u> a ground-breaking operation . . .

   A ground-breaking operation <u>was performed</u> by surgeons . . .

It's possible to form the passive using 'get' and 'have', although these are sometimes referred to as 'pseudo' passives. The 'get' passive is not generally considered appropriate in formal writing, although it's common in speech and informal writing.

I <u>got expelled</u> from school for bad behaviour.

I <u>had</u> my hair <u>coloured</u> by the salon's top stylist.

(Take care not to confuse a 'have' passive with the perfect form, which also uses 'have/had'.)

Teaching about the passive voice

Pupils are taught about active and passive at key stage 2, but there's an opportunity to reinforce and extend this further at key stage 3. We've already seen that the active voice is more frequently used than the passive, so pupils need to understand when and why they might make a conscious choice to use the passive to present information in their writing.

Once pupils understand how to recognise and form the passive, the most important thing is to explore its effect. The active voice tends to place greater emphasis on the agent, whereas the passive tends to foreground the actual action or event. Importantly, the passive allows a writer to hide, or omit the agent: this is referred to as an 'agentless passive'.

Writers might choose to use the passive for the following reasons.

1. To build suspense in narrative writing by hiding the agent:

• The french windows <u>had been left</u> slightly ajar and the curtains were fluttering in the breeze.

2. When the agent is either unknown or unimportant:

• Potassium <u>was added</u> to the test tube.

3. To sound authoritative and convincing:

• Your fitness <u>can be improved</u> in just three weeks!

4. To avoid responsibility or blame for an action:

• A controversial decision <u>was taken</u> yesterday to approve planning permission for 175 new homes in this rural village.

5. For succinctness, typically in newspaper headlines (the verb 'be' is implied):

• Woman <u>questioned</u> over plinth vandalism!

6. To create a more impersonal style:

• It <u>is believed</u> that polar bear numbers are diminishing because of global warming.

You might explore a text that makes extensive use of the passive and consider its effect.

> A sculpture displayed on Trafalgar Square's fourth plinth <u>was defaced</u> yesterday with red spray paint. The sculpture <u>had</u> only recently <u>been selected</u> for display on the plinth, which <u>is used</u> to display contemporary works on a temporary basis. Experts <u>will be consulted</u> in the hope that the paint <u>can be removed</u> without damaging the artwork further. A woman <u>is being questioned</u>.

Similarly, you might explore the use of the active voice. In the following report, the predominant use of the active emphasises the force of the storm whereas a single passive is used to present the victims.

> Hurricane force winds tore through the Caribbean last night, destroying property and leaving thousands homeless. The storm, which gained in intensity as it ripped across the Atlantic, reached the islands in the early hours when most local people were in bed. Victims of the storm <u>are being cared for</u> by the emergency services and charity organisations.

What you need to know about multi-clause sentences

A sentence can be made up of a single clause or multiple clauses.

A single-clause sentence typically consists of a subject and a finite (tensed) verb, as well as other elements. As a main clause, it can stand on its own as a sentence.

- I can't swim.
- Molly frantically searched under her bed, through her chest of drawers and in her wardrobe.

Co-ordinated clauses are clauses that have the same grammatical status as each other (either main or subordinate, but not mixed). They are typically joined by a co-ordinating conjunction. A sentence that consists of main clauses joined by co-ordinating conjunctions is sometimes referred to as a compound sentence. Of course, sentences can contain multiple co-ordination – in other words, they can contain more than two co-ordinated clauses:

- Joe wanted to see a film <u>and</u> then go for a meal, <u>but</u> it was getting late <u>and</u> I wanted an early night.

Although their prime function is to join clauses, co-ordinating conjunctions can be used for stylistic effect to start a sentence, although this is generally less typical in more formal writing.

- He couldn't contemplate stealing from his best friend. Or could he?

Subordinate clauses are sometimes referred to as dependent clauses – they can't make a complete sentence on their own, but contribute their meaning to a main (or independent) clause. In the following sentences, the subordinate clauses are underlined):

- We stayed indoors all day <u>because it was pouring with rain</u>.
- <u>If it's sunny tomorrow</u>, we might go to the beach.
- We stayed up talking <u>until it was late</u>.
- The idea <u>that I wanted her job</u> is completely absurd.

Subordinate clauses are typically introduced by a subordinating conjunction, although they can also be introduced by a non-finite verb. And they're quite mobile, so you can position them in front of, in the middle of, or after a main clause.

Many grammarians refer to sentences containing one or more subordinate clauses as complex sentences. Although this is an established grammatical term, it can give the impression that the meaning conveyed by the sentence is complex, which is not necessarily the case. Similarly, a sentence that consists of a single clause is sometimes referred to as a simple sentence, even though its structure and the ideas it conveys may not be simple at all. Consider the following:

I went to bed early as I was exhausted.	'Complex' sentence containing a subordinate clause (as I was exhausted).
The teacher carefully reversed her brand-new sports car into the very last space in the school car park.	'Simple' sentence containing a single clause (there is only one verb: reversed).

For this reason, many people prefer to refer to single-clause and multi-clause sentences (and this is also the terminology used in the primary national curriculum).

Teaching about multi-clause sentences

Pupils are taught about co-ordination and subordination at key stages 1 and 2. One of the growth points at secondary is to teach them how to deploy layers of co-ordination and subordination in multi-clause sentences.

One of the best ways to teach this is through active demonstration – or modelling. This isn't the same as showing pupils an example (or a model) – it's where you actually demonstrate the writing process, 'thinking aloud' as you write, deliberating on and orally rehearsing the choices you make as a writer. When appropriate, you can invite pupils to share the composition with you, sifting and evaluating their contributions as you continue to compose the writing together. It's sometimes called 'shared writing' and the beauty of it is that it demystifies the writing process, making it highly visible.

Another advantage is that you can model relatively short pieces of writing. For example, you can demonstrate how layers of meaning and detail can be built up in a single sentence through multiple layers of co-ordination and subordination:

The cyclist could have won the race	(main clause)
when his main opponent pulled out	(subordinate clause introduced by 'when')
but he was disqualified	(clause introduced by co-ordinating conjunction 'but')
after he broke the takeover rules	(subordinate clause introduced by 'after')
forcing another rider off the track	(non-finite subordinate clause introduced by non-finite verb 'forcing')
and almost causing a serious injury.	(non-finite clause introduced by non-finite verb 'causing' and linked to previous clause by co-ordinating conjunction 'and')

You could try the same with the following:

> The swimmers fastened their goggles
>
> and dived into the sea
>
> paying no heed to the rough waves
>
> until they reached the shore
>
> where they heaved themselves up the beach
>
> and collapsed onto the sand.

This is also a good opportunity to explore the effect of fronting or embedding clauses as well as the appropriate use of commas (a single comma is typically used to buffer the fronted subordinate clause from the main clause, and a pair of commas is typically used to buffer an embedded subordinate clause from the main clause).

What you need to know about sentence variety

Sentence variety is an essential element in effective writing, so it's a really important skill to teach pupils. Sentences can be varied in a number of ways:

1. Varying sentence length – for example, by combining a short, single-clause sentence with longer sentences for dramatic impact:

> I crept out of bed and down the stairs, pausing on my parents' landing to make sure they weren't awake. I hesitated. I tiptoed on to the hallway when I thought I heard a sound. The oak front door should have been closed and bolted by my father before he retired to bed. But it was ajar . . .

2. Varying sentence structure – for example, by fronting or embedding a subordinate clause or an adverbial:

> On the bottom of the sea bed, in the depths of the deepest ocean, lurks the giant squid. Its tentacles, undulating in the current, seem to beckon. As it slowly emerges from its lair, it ambushes its unsuspecting prey.

3. Varying clause types – for example, by using co-ordination or subordination, or a combination of the two, or by using a single-clause sentence for stylistic effect:

> The comedian stood in the wings, waiting his turn. It was not unusual for him to be physically sick before a show and tonight was no exception. Just as the lights went up and the crowd began to roar, he hesitated. Then he strode onto the stage.

4. Varying sentence forms so that they fulfil different functions (remember that it's the <u>main clause</u> in a sentence that determines its form):

Declaratives (typically associated with statements)	• The figure stood there, beckoning to me to follow. • People on Orkney refer to the Northern Lights as the Merry Dancers . . .
Interrogatives (typically associated with questions, including rhetorical questions)	• Can you imagine a more terrifying sight? • Why not consider a cruise round the Hebridean Islands?
Exclamatives (typically associated with exclamations)	• How I wish I'd never set eyes on the wretched place! • What an amazing experience that was!
Imperatives (typically associated with commands)	• Don't forget to lock and bolt the door! • Visit the Shetland Isles and see the spectacular Northern Lights.

Teaching about sentence variety

Pupils are taught about statements, questions, exclamations and commands at key stages 1 and 2, but they probably won't be familiar with the terminology declaratives, interrogatives, exclamatives or imperatives.

Different types of writing, depending on purpose and intended audience, are likely to deploy sentence forms in different ways – they may well depend more heavily on some than others. It's helpful to explore this with pupils in the context of their own reading and writing:

- Fictional narrative typically tells a story, portrays character and creates atmosphere, so it's likely to consist largely of declaratives. However, interrogatives, exclamatives and imperatives may well appear in dialogue.
- Writing that gives information or provides commentary, such as travel writing, biography or journalistic articles, is also likely to employ declaratives (the most commonly used sentence form), perhaps with some interrogatives (Can you imagine a more intoxicating sight?) and exclamatives (How enchanting the little hill town was, with its cobbled streets, whitewashed houses and flowering bougainvillea!) to engage the reader and convey the writer's stance. In straightforward information or explanation writing, interrogatives may appear as sub-headings followed by declaratives providing information in the form of answers.
- Writing that instructs or advises, such as guidance documents, recipes or instructions, is likely to depend largely on imperatives, although there may be the occasional declarative to explain why a procedure is necessary (The sun can be very damaging to your skin so it's important to protect it).
- Writing that aims to persuade or inspire the reader, such as political speeches, promotional leaflets or campaign material, may well draw on the full range of sentence forms: declaratives to give information, interrogatives (including rhetorical questions) to address the audience, exclamatives to express strong feeling, and imperatives to influence opinion and behaviour.

The literature texts you're studying should provide plenty of opportunities to teach about sentence variety. For example, you might explore the final chapter of *Lord of the Flies*, immediately before the appearance of the naval officer, when Ralph is running for his life, hunted down by the other boys. Golding skilfully deploys a range of sentence structures: single-clause sentences interspersed with multi-clause sentences vividly create the urgency of Ralph's panic and desperation; non-finite –ing verbs create the sense of never-ending pursuit and terror; and the more matter of fact style used by Golding to present the naval officer provides a stark contrast, reminding the reader that these are – after all – just little boys.

This sort of focused attention on a short passage – perhaps by annotating it on the whiteboard or visualiser to make the process visible to the class – can attune pupils to the way writers use language, alerting them to the way sentence variety can impact on the reader. This is important learning that pupils will carry over into their own writing as well as to other reading.

What you need to know about narrative voice and viewpoint

As writers, we can determine the perspective – or point of view – of our writing voice. We can choose to write in the first person, the second person or the third person. We also have a choice of singular or plural. We typically distinguish between first person, second person and third person through our choice of pronouns.

First person pronouns	I/me/mine/my/myself (singular) We/us/ours/our/ourselves (plural)
Second person pronouns	You/yours/your/yourself (singular) You/yours/your/yourselves (plural)
Third person pronouns	He/him/his/himself/she/hers/her/herself/it/its/itself (singular) They/them/theirs/their/themselves (plural)

The first person is used when the subject is speaking or writing about itself or from its own perspective, using first person pronouns.

- I woke up this morning and knew straightaway that something was terribly wrong. My phone started to ring and I answered it, immediately fearing the worst.

- We've campaigned vigorously for the protection of endangered species, and our determination to eradicate poaching is now greater than ever.

The second person is used to directly address the reader, using second person pronouns. It's not commonly used in narrative, but is often used in persuasive writing.

- How would you feel if you were shut up in a tiny cage all day with no food or water?

- Well, you never know when you're going to need a piece of chicken wire. That's why you should never throw things away . . .

The third person is used to refer to a third party (i.e. not the writer or the reader). Third person pronouns are used, as well as nouns, noun phrases and proper names.

- The rain fell in torrents and Mikey gazed out of the window. It was only the second day of the holidays and he was already bored.

Here's a quick reminder about some different types of pronouns. Personal pronouns have both a subject and an object form:

Subject personal pronouns	Object personal pronouns
I, you, he, she, it, we, you, they	me, you, him, her, it, us, you, them

Possessive pronouns indicate ownership (or possession). They are classed as either possessive pronouns or possessive determiners (also referred to as possessive adjectives). **Reflexive pronouns** refer back to (or reflect) the subject of the clause: compare <u>Tim helped him</u> to <u>Tim helped himself</u>.

Possessive pronouns	Possessive determiners	Reflexive pronouns
mine, yours, his, hers, ours, yours, theirs	my, your, his, her, its, our, your, their	myself, yourself, himself, herself, itself, ourselves, yourselves, themselves

In more formal or impersonal writing, the personal pronoun 'one' can be used to refer to people more generically (e.g. One should not be unduly concerned about the recent rise in violent crime).

In speech and more informal writing, the second person 'you' tends to be used (You can usually pick up some good bargains at the market).

Teaching about narrative voice and viewpoint

Pupils are taught about pronouns at key stage 2 – in particular, the way they support cohesion by avoiding unnecessary repetition. At secondary, there's a great opportunity to build on this by exploring the way pronouns can express narrative voice and viewpoint in literature.

A first-person narrative lets the reader see things through the eyes of the narrator. While this can enable the reader to identify more closely with the narrator, this type of narration can be limiting (or unreliable), as the reader only ever knows as much as the narrator.

Third-person narratives can feel more impersonal, as if a disembodied narrator is describing the thoughts and feelings of the characters. This type of narrator is all-seeing – or omniscient – and can tell or show the reader things that the characters don't necessarily know themselves. However, some writers choose to use a 'limited' third person narrator to reveal events through the perspective of a particular character.

To demonstrate the effect of adopting different viewpoints, you might ask pupils to rewrite a well-known or traditional tale from different perspectives. Here's how it might work with 'Little Red Riding Hood':

- I knew it would be a bad idea to visit Granny today. She started behaving strangely from the minute she opened the door. And she didn't seem at all bothered about the basket of goodies we'd gone to the trouble of packing for her . . .
- Now you know you shouldn't dawdle in the forest, especially not when there are wolves on the prowl. So when you spot some pretty flowers, and you're tempted to stop and pick them – you really shouldn't!
- He was hungry. He hadn't eaten for days. So when he was woken by a chubby little girl picking flowers just outside his den, he wondered whether fortune just might, at long last, be smiling on him.

Or you might explore multiple narration and shifts in narrative voice. For example, in the novel *Stone Cold*, Robert Swindells tells the story from the point of view of two different first-person narrators, cleverly interweaving the narratives so that the reader sees more than a single perspective.

Moving beyond fictional narrative, you might explore the use of viewpoint in persuasive writing:

- The first person can make the reader feel included and implicated in the action. (How can we allow these habitats to be destroyed?)
- The second person can address the reader directly. (Did you know that plants found in rainforests are used in modern medicines?)
- The third person can present facts. (Rainforests help to regulate the world's weather patterns.)

Or you could teach pupils about a group of adverbs called disjuncts that indicate a writer's stance or viewpoint:

- <u>Personally</u>, I don't care whether you buy it or not.
- She was, <u>surprisingly</u>, on time!
- <u>Fortunately</u>, the woodsman heard the cries and ran to the cottage.
- Our offer was, <u>disappointingly</u>, refused.

What you need to know about style

Style makes things distinctive, and writing is no exception. If you have a favourite writer, you may be so in tune with the way they choose their words, structure their sentences and employ narrative voice, that you're able to recognise their particular writing style.

Style in writing is inherently linked to context, audience and purpose. For example, an article for a medical journal will adopt a quite different style to a tabloid newspaper article reporting a recent health scare.

Large organisations often have their own 'style guides' that set out their accepted or preferred usage – or 'house' style – usually because they're looking for consistency rather than individual stylistic flourishes in their corporate publications.

No doubt you've encountered books that deal with grammatical style. Sometimes these can seem quite pedantic, as they tend to express the writer's personal preferences. For example, some writers are offended by split infinitives, whereas most people nowadays regard them as not only acceptable, but sometimes preferable to the alternative.

Style relates to many of the aspects of grammar that we've already touched on in this book, such as the following.

VOCABULARY CHOICES

- Noun-heavy and nominalised
- Subject-specific words
- Words that connote hidden meanings and associations
- Informal and colloquial vocabulary
- More formal vocabulary choices
- Repetition or patterning of words

SENTENCE VARIETY

- Fronted and embedded clauses
- Single-clause or multi-clause sentences
- Clause types such as imperatives or interrogatives
- Non-finite clauses
- Sentence 'fragments'

VOICE AND VIEWPOINT

- Active and passive voice
- First, second and third person
- Direct address to the reader
- Levels of formality

LITERARY AND RHETORICAL DEVICES

- Figurative language (e.g. extended metaphor, pathetic fallacy, symbolism)
- Appeal to the senses
- Emotive language
- Rhetorical questions
- Patterning or repetition

Teaching about style

'Table wanted for old lady with wooden legs.' We've all heard this old joke, but it's important to teach pupils how to make their meaning clear and unambiguous. You might teach them about 'misplaced modifiers' and 'dangling participles'. For example, what's wrong with the following?

- We walked to the park with a picnic basket. (Is it a park with a picnic basket?)
- I saw the crowd in the field holding banners. (Is the field or the crowd holding the banners?)
- After playing in the garden, my father told me to wash my hands. (Who's been playing in the garden?)

You could have some fun with these, and other similar sentences. Get pupils to draw the images they bring to mind. Then get them to rewrite the sentences to make the meaning clearer.

In fictional narrative, teach pupils writerly techniques such as withholding information (I heard a noise; something was moving in the shadows), using deliberate repetition and patterning (We saw a kingfisher flitting along the riverbank; water voles nosing through the reed beds; and delicate dragonflies hunting for their prey) or using figurative language to create sensual images (The sun scorched the grass – a fierce demon scowling from on high). Encourage pupils to read back over their writing and to edit their own work. Reading their work aloud – either to themselves or to a partner – should help them to hear the sounds and patterns they've created.

You might use a sentence-combining approach. Give pupils a set of short, pithy sentences and ask them to combine them into one sentence, retaining as much of the key information as possible. You could model this first, drawing attention to the clause structures and the way you're linking them.

Here's how it might work in practice:

- We flew from the mainland
- We arrived yesterday
- We saw a stretch of coastline from the plane
- We wanted to explore the coastline
- We decided to hire a boat

> We decided to hire a boat and explore the stretch of coastline that we'd spied from the plane when we flew in from the mainland the day before.

As part of literature study, you might focus on visual images by getting pupils to draw the mental pictures created by the text. Or give them words and fragments from a text (a 'reverse cloze' activity) to draw attention to a writer's themes and preoccupations. Alternatively, if you've been reading a novel by an author with a particularly distinctive style, ask pupils to write an additional chapter or an alternative ending in the same style. Or you might take a well-known traditional tale and ask pupils to rewrite it in the style of a different genre, such as crime fiction, gothic horror, science fiction or romantic fiction:

- Goldie had been in trouble for breaking and entering before, but she'd never done porridge for sleeping in someone else's bed . . .
- A strange howl rang out in the darkness as a little girl with long blonde hair trotted through the woods. She was late – and lost. Was that a cottage between the trees? And was that a light glowing in its window?

What you need to know about structure and cohesion

The way a text is structured will vary according to the type of writing, its purpose and intended reader or audience. This applies not only to the way the whole text is organised, but also to its internal cohesion.

Narratives, such as novels, stories and plays – which are typically based on conflict – tend to follow a core structure: an opening or exposition in which the conflict or dilemma is established, a rising action leading to the climax (sometimes with a complication or crisis en route), and a falling action moving towards final resolution. There may also be inter-connected sub-plots.

The underlying organising principle in narrative is chronology, yet a skilled writer won't necessarily reveal events to the reader in this way. Writers may employ shifts in time – such as flashbacks, time shifts and foreshadowing of key events – as well as shifts in perspective such as multiple narration. Structural devices might include the way the writer positions details for effect, such as a cliffhanger at the end of a chapter or episode to create tension or suspense. Paragraphs can be used to signal a change in time (As the months passed . . .; The following day . . .) or perspective (While Jamie was looking out of the window, Sara was . . .), or to indicate that a different character is speaking in dialogue.

In non-chronological writing, shape and structure are likely to be determined by purpose and form. For example, a balanced argument might start with an opening paragraph that introduces the issue, followed by further paragraphs each dealing with a single argument either for or against the issue. Alternatively, each paragraph might deal with one argument and its supporting evidence, followed by the counter argument with further supporting evidence. Paragraphs are likely to include a topic sentence clearly signalling the main argument under consideration, followed by supporting evidence and further elaboration. A concluding paragraph then draws the arguments together, perhaps by including the writer's own recommendation or opinion.

Cohesion relates to the way a text is knitted together, with cohesive features acting as signposts to steer the reader through the text. These may include any of the following:

- Conjunctions and adverbials (<u>While</u> some residents feel <u>that</u> the flooding could have been prevented <u>and</u> are demanding answers from their local MP, members of the community are <u>nevertheless</u> supporting each other <u>as</u> the full extent of the devastation caused by last week's torrential rainfall becomes apparent.)

- Pronouns (The duchess was greeted by a crowd of cheering children who presented <u>her</u> with a huge bouquet of flowers. As <u>she</u> shook hands with the headteacher, <u>everybody</u> commented on how well <u>she</u> looked. <u>This</u> was the most memorable day of the year for the small village school.)

- Determiners (<u>These</u> endangered species will soon be extinct unless <u>this</u> government acts now to stop <u>the</u> poaching.)

- Ellipsis (Sally is a strong swimmer but her sister isn't [a strong swimmer].)

- Thematic linkage, including deliberate repetition and synonyms (The <u>starving</u> children are piteous to behold; their <u>hunger</u> is etched on their <u>gaunt</u> faces as their <u>food supplies</u> are all but <u>exhausted</u>.)

Teaching about structure and cohesion

It's important for pupils to understand the constructed nature of text, whether it's fiction or non-fiction, prose or poetry. Unlike in real life, every detail, including where it's positioned in a text, has significance. When a writer lays a clue or drops a hint, there's a reason: to hook or prepare the reader, to deepen understanding of a particular character or event, or to gradually build an argument to its conclusion.

The way a text is shaped is key to its effectiveness, so it's important to teach pupils how to plan. (Don't take it for granted that they know how to do this.) Planning is as much about thinking as it is about writing and, for many pupils, it can be a way of getting over the fear of the 'blank page'. There's no single way to go about planning: it will vary according to the type of text being written as well as to personal preference. For example, a narrative might lend itself to a storyboard, a story mountain or a flow chart. For texts that aren't structured chronologically, such as argument, persuasion or critical evaluation, you might use a mind map, an argument tree, a spidergram or a 'for and against' grid. It's important that a plan is not seen as a constraint: as their writing progresses, pupils can amend or refine their original thinking. Effective planning enables a writer to order their thoughts, but it also allows them to add in or prune back, selecting or rejecting ideas. Without some form of planning, there's a risk that the end product could lack shape and structure.

Check that pupils understand how to organise their ideas into paragraphs. Research by the Qualifications and Curriculum Authority (QCA) some years ago revealed that many pupils at key stage 3 saw paragraphing as simply a layout feature – something visual that broke up a page. Teach pupils how to craft a paragraph and to link one paragraph to another. Help them to understand that paragraphs can't be teased out retrospectively if they're not constructed in the first place.

There are plenty of opportunities to explore structure and cohesion in reading and writing. You might explore the structure of a short non-fiction text, looking at the way important points are foregrounded or juxtapositioned; the way the opening and ending are linked; or the way thematic linkage creates semantic chains, linking word choice to meaning.

You might explore the way pronouns can refer forwards to a noun or noun phrase (known as cataphoric reference), as well as backwards (known as anaphoric reference). Cataphoric reference is a particularly useful technique to teach your pupils when they want to create an element of intrigue in their writing. In the following example, notice how the noun (Davinia) is withheld to create interest and an element of suspense:

- As she slowly descended the staircase, her gown trailing behind her, all eyes were upon her: Davinia certainly knew how to make an entrance!

In literature, you might look at the way different storylines are woven together and the order in which they're resolved, discussing how this provides a satisfying ending – or not – for the reader. You might ask pupils to trace a theme throughout a novel, or to work out how a character's backstory is pieced together. Ask them to predict the ending of a short story, and then track back to see how the writer has prepared the reader for the actual ending. Or give pupils a pivotal section from a novel they're studying, ask them to pick out a handful of key events and use them to draw a tension graph to show how the placing of particular details builds tension. They could then use this as a planning tool for their own writing.

Chapter 3
Punctuation for meaning and effect

What you need to know about punctuation for meaning and effect

Punctuation marks separate sentences and the elements contained within them (such as graphemes, words, phrases and clauses) and their primary function is to clarify meaning. We punctuate writing to guide our reader, to help them navigate and make sense of our writing.

Grammar and punctuation are so closely integrated that it would seem strange not to include a chapter on punctuation in this book. The companion primary book, *Grammar Survival for Primary Teachers*, deals with the main forms of punctuation that are taught in the primary years; in this book, we'll focus more on punctuation for meaning and effect: separating grammatical units in a sentence, indicating parenthetical information, conveying shades of subtlety, and avoiding ambiguity in writing.

We'll also recap aspects of basic punctuation that some of your pupils may not have completely secured, such as the use of the apostrophe and speech punctuation as well as common errors such as the comma splice.

Punctuation is perhaps best seen as a set of conventions. Although there are rules, there is still disagreement about some of them, such as the use of the serial (or 'Oxford' comma). And much punctuation usage does come down to personal and stylistic choice – for example, whether we favour a 'heavy' or 'light' approach to punctuation. Numerous style guides have their say too.

Some punctuation continues to confuse writers well into adulthood (think of the 'greengrocer's apostrophe' where highly visible errors such as <u>Jersey Royal potato's</u> invite criticism and lead to talk about falling standards). Sometimes we take a more liberal approach to punctuation: text messaging often leaves out punctuation completely, as does some critically renowned poetry. However, if we're going to break the rules or adapt the conventions for literary and creative effect, or simply for economy, we need to know what they are in the first place.

When you're teaching about punctuation, it's important to remember the following:

- Punctuation, like grammar, is best taught in the context of writing, rather than through decontextualised exercises. This way, we can keep the focus on the way it supports the reader's understanding.

- It's important for pupils to know when punctuation is just right or wrong (for example, the punctuation of speech, the demarcation of a sentence, or the use of an apostrophe) and when they have a choice. For example, punctuation choices can convey formality (semi-colons and colons can look impressive in letters of application) or informality (dashes and exclamation marks are often associated with more informal writing).

- Editing and proof-reading have a vital part to play. Some writers prefer to punctuate during the process of composition; others prefer to go back and refine the punctuation once a section has been drafted. Either way, the writer needs to be the first proof-reader of the writing, taking responsibility for checking that their intended meaning is clear.

- The way we respond to punctuation in pupils' writing is key; simply making corrections without providing some kind of explanation for the error, or giving feedback such as 'check your punctuation', is unlikely to lead to any significant improvement.

Teaching about punctuation: recapping the basics

The full range of punctuation is taught during the primary years, but some of your pupils may have transferred to secondary with gaps in their understanding. It's important that you know whether errors in their writing are as a result of this, or simply a lack of careful proofing. There are three aspects of punctuation that you'll want to address urgently if they're not being used correctly:

1.   Marking sentence boundaries

There are likely to be two main issues: forgetting to use full stops to mark sentence boundaries (Mike is a very good swimmer he trains every day) or using a comma to mark sentence boundaries – otherwise known as 'comma splicing' (Mike is a very good swimmer, he trains every day). Both examples in brackets are <u>incorrect</u>.

Some errors are likely to be the result of inadequate proofing, so make it a non-negotiable expectation that pupils always edit their own writing before sharing it with other readers.

If it's not a proofing issue, and pupils genuinely don't understand how to demarcate sentence boundaries, then you need to revisit clause structure and explain that a comma isn't strong enough to separate two independent clauses. Show pupils the alternatives:

*   John is a very good swimmer. He trains every day. (Use a full stop and start a new sentence.)
*   John is a very good swimmer because he trains every day. (Use a conjunction.)
*   John is a very good swimmer; he trains every day. (Use a semi-colon.)
*   John is a very good swimmer – he trains every day. (Use a dash.)
*   John is a very good swimmer: he trains every day. (If appropriate, use a colon.)

2.   Using apostrophes

If pupils are making mistakes with apostrophes, it's likely to be a result of misunderstanding. You'll need to pinpoint the specific misconception – simply correcting the errors in a pupil's writing is likely to make little difference if they don't know how to use them.

You might need to remind pupils of the following:

*   Straightforward plural words where there is no possession do not take an apostrophe (the dog's are barking = an error).
*   In a contracted form, the apostrophe goes where the letter or letters have been missed out and not necessarily where the words are joined (would'nt = an error).
*   It's, they're and who's are all contracted forms.

If pupils are struggling with apostrophes for possession and can't work out whether to put the apostrophe before or after the 's', ask them who owns what. There are likely to be two nouns together, the first one being the owner. Put the apostrophe straight after the name of the owner. You could model this first, sharing your thought process. 'Does this show possession? Yes, but who owns what? OK – the books belong to the children, which means I need to put the apostrophe straight after 'children' and before the 's' – like this: I put the <u>children's books</u> back on the shelf.'

3.   Indicating direct speech

Pupils should know that inverted commas go around the spoken words, but you may need to remind them how to punctuate a reporting clause. The best way is to look at some examples and ask them what happens if the spoken words are interrupted by some unspoken words and what they notice about where the comma goes. Reinforce this whenever they write dialogue until it's secure.

If only a handful of pupils are struggling with these aspects, consider working with a small guided writing group so that you can really monitor any misunderstandings and intervene to support pupils.

What you need to know about commas to separate grammatical units in a sentence

Since most dictionary definitions of punctuation make reference to the marks that separate sentences and their elements, we do need to consider the way punctuation relates to grammar. We've already seen that commas don't have the power to separate sentences: instead, they work within sentences, separating words, phrases and clauses in lists, and 'buffering' grammatical units such as phrases and clauses from other elements in the sentence.

There are very few 'hard and fast' rules about commas, but there are some generally accepted conventions about their use to separate phrases and clauses from other parts of the sentence.

A comma is typically used to mark off a fronted adverbial from the rest of the sentence:

- Sadly, I won't be able to make it this evening.
- Shortly before midnight, the bells started to chime.
- Without giving him a second glance, Sally walked away.
- Startled by the fireworks, the cows stampeded across the field.
- Just as we sat down to eat, the telephone rang.

However, it's not essential to use a comma after a fronted adverbial. If the adverbial is short and the meaning is clear, it may not be necessary:

- Today I must start my literature essay.
- This time next week we'll be on holiday.

Fronted subordinate clauses are typically marked by a comma; similarly, subordinate clauses that are dropped into the middle of a main clause are typically buffered by a pair of commas:

- Since it was getting late, the head teacher decided to finish the meeting early.
- The head teacher, since it was getting late, decided to finish the meeting early.

However, it's not usually necessary to put a comma after a fronted main clause unless it supports clarity:

- The head teacher decided to finish the meeting early since it was getting late.
- The oystercatchers stood silhouetted on the shoreline, facing into the wind.

Sometimes we insert a comma after a main clause when it's followed by a conjunction of contrast, such as <u>but</u>, <u>although</u> or <u>while</u>:

- My friends weren't keen, but I really wanted to go to the concert.
- Liam is training for a marathon, while I prefer more gentle exercise.

The longer the clause, the more likely it is that a comma will help to orientate the reader:

- We headed up into the hills on a narrow, winding, unmade road, and marvelled at the mountain views.

The shorter the clause, and the greater the cohesion between the clauses, the less likely it is that a comma is needed:

- Tom loved football and he played every Saturday.

We'll look at commas to mark relative clauses in a separate section.

Teaching about commas to separate grammatical units in a sentence

To make the point about the importance of commas, give pupils a passage without any and ask them to discuss how the absence of commas affects the way they read it. Then ask them to insert commas into the most appropriate places and compare their choices. You could use the passage below.

> St Ives a seaside town and fishing port in Cornwall is inundated with tourists during the summer months. Owing to its popularity the best way to visit the town is by train as parking in the town is limited and the streets are typically congested a problem exacerbated by the large numbers that descend on the pretty town every year.
>
> Renowned for its art galleries including the famous Tate St Ives which opened in 1993 it is the home of many painters and sculptors. Just west of St Ives several miles out to sea lies Seal Island home to a small colony of Grey Atlantic Seals.

If you want to secure pupils' understanding of the way commas 'buffer' fronted and embedded subordinate clauses from other elements, you could use an investigative approach. Give pupils a number of sentences and ask them to work out why some use commas, while others do not. You'll need enough examples for the rule to be apparent so that pupils can generalise from the examples given. This is a good way to surface pupils' implicit understanding, making it explicit. Ask them to agree a simple explanation to secure their learning.

After he had finished his book, Robin turned out the light.	She forgot to pick up her keys before she slammed the door.
I'll clear away the dishes if you help me.	I swim every week, even when I'm busy, as it's a good way to keep fit.
Once he started college, Philip made lots of new friends.	Sini peered in the shop window while she waited for her brother.
Although the puppy had been trained, it still barked loudly whenever the doorbell rang.	Even though it was getting late, they decided to walk home from the cinema.
Janice, since leaving home, had started to appreciate her mother's cooking.	We might, if it stops raining, think about going for a walk.

Draw attention to pupils' use of commas in a short section of their own writing, be it a literary essay or a piece of narrative fiction. This will support the transfer of knowledge to application by encouraging pupils to build a specific feature into their own work having previously practised it in a more focused way.

What you need to know about punctuation to indicate parenthetical information

When we talk about something being 'in parenthesis', we're referring to a word or group of words inserted into a sentence as a kind of afterthought, rather like an 'aside' in a play. We usually punctuate parenthetical words by a pair of brackets, dashes or commas. (The term 'parentheses' can also be used to describe a pair of brackets.)

The words in parenthesis usually provide additional, non-essential information and could be removed without affecting the sense of the sentence:

- This poem (written by Heaney in memory of his mother) is one of the most memorable in the anthology.

- This poem – written by Heaney in memory of his mother – is one of the most memorable in the anthology.

- This poem, written by Heaney in memory of his mother, is one of the most memorable in the anthology.

While we have a choice of using brackets, dashes or commas, we need to know that they can have slightly different effects in our writing. Brackets and dashes tend to mark a stronger interruption, whereas commas tend to mark a weaker interruption which can appear more integrated into the sentence:

- The Battle of the Somme (one of the most senseless and deadly battles of the First World War) was commemorated on its centenary in July 2016.

- The decision to build the new road is – in my opinion – an absolute disaster.

- This year's school play was, as always, a great success.

Dashes tend to be used in more informal writing, as they can create a spontaneous, speechlike effect:

- She came running downstairs to answer the phone – I'd repeatedly told her the stair carpet was dangerous – and twisted her ankle.

A pair of brackets can enclose a complete sentence that's not part of another sentence. When we do this, the end punctuation goes inside the brackets:

- The theatre trip was, as always, a great success. (This year, we went to see *Hamlet*.)

While brackets and dashes can mark off a complete main clause, a pair of commas can only mark off a subordinate clause, a phrase or a word:

- The train arrived, fortunately, just in time.
- We completed the day's hike, sweating profusely, and decided to go for a swim.

Although brackets, dashes and commas are used in pairs to indicate parenthesis, you can also use a single dash to indicate a parenthetical afterthought when it falls at the end of a sentence:

- We're planning an arts festival this year – an event that promises to be a great success.

Teaching about punctuation to indicate parenthetical information

It's well worth teaching pupils how to drop additional (parenthetical) information into a sentence, as this enables a writer to convey detail economically, without the need for additional sentences. Of course, it's also important to teach them how to use appropriate punctuation to show the reader that this additional information can be removed without affecting the meaning.

You'll be able to link punctuation for parenthesis with work on relative clauses. (Remember that non-defining [non-restrictive] relative clauses provide additional information that is not essential to the meaning.)

Typically, a pair of commas is used around a non-defining (non-restrictive) relative clause, but a pair of brackets or dashes could be used instead. If pupils are familiar with non-defining relative clauses, it's worth exploring the different effects of using commas, dashes or brackets:

- My nephew, who was of a sunny disposition, came to stay with me every summer.
- My nephew – who was of a sunny disposition – came to stay with me every summer.
- My nephew (who was of a sunny disposition) came to stay with me every summer.

The logical next step is to show them how other words, phrases and clauses can be used parenthetically. Try using a sentence-combining approach. Give pupils a number of short sentences that provide information about a given topic. Ask them to combine them into two or three longer sentences, retaining as much of the key information as possible and using appropriate punctuation. You could model this first, drawing attention to the clause structures and the way you're linking them. Punctuation choices should provide an important focus for discussion.

Many young people like to travel.	There are many wonderful places to see in the world.
There are many reasons why travel is popular.	Travel can be expensive.
Travel can expand your horizons.	It's good to experience other cultures.
Travelling can make you more independent.	A big trip needs to be planned carefully.

> Travel is, understandably, very popular with young people. The world is full of wonderful places to visit (many with very distinctive cultures) that will expand your horizons and perspectives. Travel can be expensive though – especially if you want to see far-flung places – and trips need to be carefully planned.

In Chapter 2, we looked at noun phrases in apposition (two noun phrases positioned next to each other and referring to the same thing). When the second noun phrase gives additional (parenthetical) information about the first, they're typically separated by a comma:

- Mr Thomas, our new teacher, is organising the geography field trip this year.
- My brother, the best-selling novelist, has just published a new book.

However, when the second noun phrase specifies or defines the noun it follows (and is therefore essential to the meaning), a comma is not typically used:

- My brother John is coming over from New Zealand next month.
- I can always rely on my friend Jane when I need help.

What you need to know about punctuation to convey shades of subtlety in writing

Semi-colons and colons are really useful punctuation marks that can convey subtleties of meaning with economy and precision.

A semi-colon can join two independent clauses. It's stronger than a comma, yet not as abrupt as a full stop. It joins two clauses that are closely related in meaning, creating a sense of balance and co-ordination, and establishing a semantic link – which the reader has to work out – between the two clauses.

- The door hung lopsidedly on one hinge; the plaster was crumbling and damp.
- Clare was reading; Tom was chatting.

Of course, you could just write two separate sentences, or use a conjunction to join the two clauses. However, the effect would be different in each case.

- Claire was reading. Tom was chatting.
- Claire was reading, but Tom was chatting.
- Claire was reading so Tom was chatting.
- Claire was reading while Tom was chatting.

Semi-colons can also be used to separate items in more complex lists, where commas wouldn't make the meaning sufficiently clear, as in the example below. Notice the semi-colon before the final 'and'.

> We saw a kingfisher flitting along the riverbank, a flash of bright blue in the sunlight; water voles nosing their way through the reed beds, heading for their burrows; and delicate dragonflies, hunting for their prey.

Like the semi-colon, a colon can also join two independent clauses, typically where the second clause provides some explanation, elaboration or clarification of the first. Whereas a semi-colon suggests a sense of balance, a colon works like a pair of headlamps, pointing ahead to subsequent explanation, elaboration or clarification:

- The teacher knew that Paul would do well in his exams: he had always been a most diligent student.
- Stepping into the foggy darkness, Tabitha sensed movement: a dark shape retreated into the garden.

Unlike a semi-colon, the words that follow the colon don't have to be a main clause – they may just consist of a phrase or a single word. However, the words that precede the colon are almost always a main clause:

- The school was facing a major challenge: the recruitment of a new headteacher.
- Sandra could think of only one reason for his behaviour: jealousy.

A colon can also introduce a list (notice again how it's preceded by a main clause):

- There were strong arguments in favour of the new supermarket: convenience, greater choice and lower prices.

You'll notice that, unless the colon is introducing a quotation, the words that follow it don't normally start with a capital letter unless they're proper nouns.

Teaching about punctuation to convey shades of subtlety in writing

Try teaching colons through suspense writing alongside dashes and ellipsis dots as a way of hinting at what might be coming next.

> As I ascended the staircase, a sense of foreboding filled my whole being: the door to the attic – shut and bolted only this morning – was now wide open.

These could be written as two sentences, but – like headlights – the colon helps the reader sense that something lies ahead. Demonstrate the convention, and then ask pupils to write their own suspense-filled sentences. Give them a setting: an abandoned railway station, a school building at night, or a derelict cottage.

You can teach semi-colons and colons when writing about literature – for example, when introducing a quotation. While the most effective literature essays are likely to embed short quotations into the writing itself, pupils may sometimes want to use a longer quotation, and introduce it using a colon.

The recurring images of blood in the play symbolise the guilt of Macbeth and his wife:

> 'Will all great Neptune's ocean wash this blood
>
> Clean from my hand? No, this my hand will rather
>
> The multitudinous seas incarnadine,
>
> Making the green one red.'

Take the opportunity to demonstrate punctuation choices when you're modelling writing. For example, if you're writing about the relationship between George and Lennie in *Of Mice and Men*, you can show pupils how to use a semi-colon to balance the description of the two contrasting characters. Here's an example of how this might work:

You say . . .	You write . . .
I want to start by briefly describing Lennie – I'll say three things about him . . . Notice how the semi-colon lets me set the contrasting description of George right alongside it, without the need for a new sentence or another conjunction . . .	Lennie is huge and powerful, yet childlike; George is small and quick-thinking, and takes responsibility for Lennie.
Now I need to support what I'm saying by referring to evidence in the novel. I'll make my point about Lennie, and then give the example of the way he drinks the pond water. Then I'll use a semi-colon to balance the contrasting point about George . . .	Lennie acts without thinking when he dunks his head in the pond to drink at the start of the novel; George, in contrast, checks the water first, taking responsibility for himself and his friend.
Can you see how the semi-colons let me link the two related ideas?	

If you have able writers who persist in comma splicing, teach them about colons and semi-colons, as this may well help them to control long, multi-clause sentences in their writing.

What you need to know about punctuation to avoid ambiguity

Commas and hyphens both play an important role in helping us to avoid ambiguity in our writing.

Hyphen usage seems to be constantly evolving: typically used to join words that form a single unit, they tend to be omitted once the meaning is clearly established. But if there's a risk of ambiguity, it's best to use one.

There's a generally accepted convention to hyphenate a compound modifier when it pre-modifies a noun. For example:

The well-known actor received glowing reviews for his latest performance.	The actor was well known for his roles in the theatre.
I tried to buy some sugar-free mints.	Are these mints sugar free?

Modifiers using –ly adverbs are not typically hyphenated, because there's unlikely to be any ambiguity (A scruffily dressed individual was seen running down the lane).

The position of a comma can completely change the meaning in a sentence. This is most apparent in the case of relative clauses. A pair of commas is always used around a non-defining (non-restrictive) relative clause. This is similar to the way we use a pair of commas for parenthesis: the relative clause provides additional information that is not essential to the meaning and could therefore be simply lifted out of the sentence without affecting its meaning. Like parenthesis, a pair of brackets or dashes could be used instead.

- My friend, who lives in London, is selling her house.
- My cousin, whose wedding we went to last year, is having a baby.

If we choose to omit the commas, we change the meaning. In the following examples, the relative clauses are defining (or restrictive) in that they specify or define the noun they follow and are essential to the meaning:

- My friend who lives in London is selling her house.
- My cousin whose wedding we went to last year is having a baby.

The relative clauses (who lives in London/whose wedding we went to last year) refer to the specific friend who lives in London rather than any other friends who live elsewhere/the specific cousin who got married last year rather than any other cousins.

The decision to use a comma to mark a fronted adverbial also needs care, as this can affect the way the sentence is construed:

- Sometimes I wonder why I'm bothering with this!
- Sometimes, I fall asleep and dream that I am flying.

Teaching about punctuation to avoid ambiguity

Give pupils examples where the use or omission of a hyphen changes the meaning. Make sure they understand the differences in meaning, and then get them to generate their own examples:

Watch out! Man-eating shark!	Watch out! Man eating shark!
The tax relief is designed to support small-landowners.	The tax relief is designed to support small landowners.
The nursery caters for four-year-old children.	The nursery caters for four year-old children.
We asked them to re-serve the hot food.	We asked them to reserve the hot food.

Ask pupils to consider the impact of the commas on the meaning of the second sentence below:

- The passengers who went down with a severe sickness bug are suing the tour operator.
- The passengers, who went down with a severe sickness bug, are suing the tour operator.

(In the first sentence, only the passengers who were sick are taking legal action; in the second sentence, all of the passengers fell ill and are suing the tour operator.)

Then get pupils to generate another pair of similar sentences.

Ask pupils to explain the difference the comma makes to the meaning in the second sentence below.

- Sam didn't go to college because he wanted to become a fashion designer.
- Sam didn't go to college, because he wanted to become a fashion designer.

In the sentence without the comma, Sam went to college for another reason. In the sentence with the comma, Sam didn't go to college at all – presumably because it didn't offer a course on fashion design.

Set a homework task in which pupils review their use of commas in their own writing. Ask them to share examples of usage where the comma either obscured or clarified their intended meaning, and agree targets for future work.

Chapter 4
Levels of formality

What you need to know about levels of formality

As writers, we make choices about our writing which are largely determined by context. There are three key considerations:

- Purpose (Why am I writing this?)
- Audience (Who am I writing this for?)
- Form (So what kind of writing would be appropriate?)

This chapter deals with the way we adapt our language according to context. There's a section on the differences between spoken and written language; Standard and non-Standard English (including using Standard English in writing and speech); and formal and informal registers. However, language is rarely simply formal or informal – it tends to sit on a continuum, which is why it's more helpful to think about levels of formality. In his memoir, *Wordstruck*, the novelist and journalist Robert MacNeil draws an analogy with clothing: for example, 'the dark-suit, serious-tie language', 'blue-jeans-and-sweat-shirt language', and 'the language of pyjamas and uncombed hair'.

Pupils will have learnt about Standard English, as well as formal and informal writing, in primary school. The challenge at secondary is to teach pupils to adapt language appropriately, according to audience and purpose, and in a wider range of more challenging contexts.

Register also needs to be mentioned here. We use this term to refer to the specific language used in particular social contexts and by specific groups or professions (for example, legal, medical or scientific) when talking or writing about their own field of interest and expertise.

In his essay, 'Standard English: What it Isn't', linguist Peter Trudgill distinguishes between register and style, with register being associated more with vocabulary, and style with the degree of formality used. This is a helpful distinction: we might consider a doctor, who is likely to use the medical register differently depending on the audience (for example, writing for peers in a medical journal, giving a lecture to first-year medical students, or explaining a diagnosis to a patient).

The main thing is that young writers should have choices: the choice to use Standard English or a regional dialect; the choice to use an informal, conversational style or a more formal register. Above all, they need to understand how to exercise these choices in the context of their talking and writing, and this will depend on the purpose and intended audience.

If pupils are only ever exposed to informal language, they will be limited as speakers and writers, unable to adapt and respond flexibly to more formal contexts, audiences and purposes. For many young people, school is the place where they are likely to be exposed to the range of opportunities – through reading and writing and talk – that equip them to become flexible language users.

Teaching about levels of formality

You could draw on pupils' implicit understanding of different levels of formality by sharing a number of fragments (such as the examples below) and asking them what they can deduce about the intended audience, purpose and context. Then ask them how they know, and tease out the language features more explicitly. This textual analysis of even short pieces of text is important as it will help pupils internalise the patterns of language and grammatical features that they can then draw on in their own writing.

You could ask pupils to place the fragments on a continuum (the most formal to the least formal), explaining and justifying their decisions. Or you might ask them to choose one fragment and continue it in the same style, adopting the same level of formality and register.

This latest offering from the Oscar-nominated director looks set to be one of her best. The action-packed storyline keeps you in suspense from the very start . . .
We are pleased to enclose a cheque for £25.99 as reimbursement for your faulty goods. Please accept our apologies for the inconvenience caused by the . . .
I would never have dreamt that I would one day be a famous musician. My family wasn't particularly well-off, and my mother held down several jobs just to make ends meet . . .
In Victorian society (the setting for 'Oliver Twist'), people were either very rich or very poor. It was not unusual for children to be sent to the workhouse, where they . . .
Had a really great time yesterday. Would love to meet up again and perhaps go for a pizza . . .
A forty-two-year-old woman was being held in police custody last night after an incident outside a supermarket in which a car was seriously damaged . . .
The magnitude of the events surrounding the explosion continues to resonate today, with members of the small community residing in fear of . . .

What you need to know about Standard and non-Standard English

- Standard English is a dialect, even though it's not linked to a particular geographical region.
- It can be spoken with any accent.
- It tends to be associated with more formal speech and writing; however, it would be possible to use Standard English in informal writing, and non-Standard English in relatively formal writing.
- There are many regional dialects that differ linguistically from Standard English. These non-Standard forms are not inferior to Standard English, neither are they 'incorrect'.
- Standard English is the dialect used in education and publishing, as well as the one that's taught to non-native learners of English. It is used globally, and carries a very definite element of social and academic prestige.

DIFFERENCES BETWEEN NON-STANDARD AND STANDARD ENGLISH

Most of the differences between non-Standard and Standard English relate to verb forms, and are typically associated with irregular verbs. There's a tendency for these to be more regularised in non-Standard English, so there isn't always a distinction between first, second and third person forms. For example:

- He <u>go</u> there every day.
- They <u>goes</u> there every week.
- I <u>were</u> expecting you hours ago.
- We <u>was</u> the best of friends when we <u>was</u> at school.

Some non-Standard forms use the base form of the verb (the infinitive form without 'to') or the –ed (past participle) form for the simple past. For example:

- He <u>give</u> it to me.
- I <u>see</u> him in the park last week.
- I <u>seen</u> you in town today.
- We always <u>done</u> our homework on time.

Some of the differences relate to the way negatives are formed, with some non-Standard forms using multiple negation ('double negatives') or the word 'ain't' to form the negative of the verbs 'be' and 'have' in the simple present. For example:

- She would<u>n't</u> do <u>nothing</u> like that.
- She did<u>n't</u> see <u>nobody</u>.
- That <u>ain't</u> fair.
- I <u>ain't</u> got <u>none</u>.

Other differences relate to the way some non-Standard forms use certain determiners and pronouns. For example:

- Pass me <u>them</u> cakes from the window.
- Those shoes <u>what</u> I like are in the sale.
- In the end, they decided to go by <u>theirselves</u>.

Teaching about Standard and non-Standard English

Teaching about Standard English is about making sure that pupils have a choice, so that they can use Standard English when they need to. Most pupils are likely to use some form of non-Standard English at home, so it's vital to be sensitive to this and respectful of it. In fact, if you teach in an area where pupils use a distinctive regional dialect, this could be a really rich source of language study, drawing on local culture and oral history.

If not, there's a wealth of novels, play scripts and poetry that recreate regional dialects, and provide rich material for study. For example, in David Almond's novel *Heaven Eyes*, some characters use Standard English and others do not. In *Sons and Lovers*, D. H. Lawrence uses both Standard English and regional dialect in dialogue to convey his characters' background and social attitudes, as in this exchange between Paul Morel, his mother and his father:

> 'It's true, mother – she hasn't,' he cried, jumping up and taking his old position on the hearthrug. 'She's never read a book in her life.'
>
> ''Er's like me,' chimed in Morel. ''Er canna see what there is i' books, ter sit borin' your nose in 'em for, nor more can I.'
>
> 'But you shouldn't say these things,' said Mrs Morel to her son.

It's generally considered appropriate to use Standard English in more formal written – and sometimes spoken – contexts. Unless a writer makes a definite choice to use a regional dialect (for example, to create a vivid sense of character or location), relatively formal writing for an unknown reader typically requires Standard English. The most important thing is for pupils to have the choice: to know the conventions of Standard English and when it's appropriate to use them.

Try creating a text where Standard English would be expected, like a news report, but include some non-Standard features. Ask pupils to discuss why the non-Standard usage feels inappropriate in this context. For example:

> The education secretary and the schools minister visited visited a school in Birmingham today where they spoke with local children. They was surprised to discover that many of the pupils what had just finished their GCSE exams had already . . .

Ask pupils to consider a range of situations and decide whether it would be necessary to use Standard English and why:

- An English literature essay
- Entries in a personal diary
- A letter of complaint about a faulty product
- A play script
- A story that incorporates authentic regional dialogue
- An email to a friend
- A conversation at break time with a group of friends
- A work-experience interview
- A report for a local newspaper
- A radio football commentary
- A television interview with a well-known local celebrity

What you need to know about the differences between spoken and written language

Written language is not the same as spoken language, as any transcript of talk will show. Talk is ephemeral and generally more spontaneous than writing; it tends to be more interactive and responsive to our listeners or audience. In contrast, writing is more permanent and can be planned and edited. As writers, we have to engage with unknown and potentially remote readers.

Like writing, talk is a productive skill, meaning that there's a cognitive load that has to be managed – for example, we need to know what to say, have an idea of how to organise our thoughts and choose our words, as well a sense of who we're speaking to and the level of formality that's likely to be appropriate. Because of this, talk tends to involve pauses, repetitions, hesitations and fillers to buy thinking time. We don't necessarily speak in sentences, but rather fragments composed of single words, phrases and clauses; we're far more likely to use strings of co-ordinated clauses than complex subordination.

In *Introducing the Grammar of Talk* (Qualifications and Curriculum Authority, 2004), Professor Ron Carter makes the case for explicitly teaching pupils about spoken language and its distinctive grammatical features, including the following.

DISCOURSE MARKERS

These act like signposts to the listener, signalling the beginning or the end of an exchange, or indicating that we're ready to move on to a new topic.

- <u>Right</u>, what's this all about?
- <u>Anyway</u>, let's have a look at this.
- <u>Okay then</u>, I'll see you next week.
- <u>Well</u>, I think that's probably all we can do right now.

DEIXIS

Deictic features depend on the immediacy of a shared context and help a speaker to orientate the listener.

- If you look <u>over there</u>, you'll see precisely what I mean.
- I'd like two of <u>these</u>, please.
- Did you see <u>that</u> programme last night, <u>the one about</u> the penguins?
- Shall we just run through <u>this</u> presentation once more?

ELLIPSIS

This involves the omission of certain grammatical elements, since the shared context means that the meaning is clear without them.

- I love swimming – always have. (I always have loved swimming.)
- Got any of your organic baked beans today? (Have you got any of your . . .)
- Sorry – too busy to stop and chat. (I'm sorry – I'm too busy to . . .)
- Phone battery's flat – I'll need to charge it before we go out. (My phone battery's flat . . .)

VAGUE LANGUAGE

This is often used deliberately to soften (or 'hedge') an exchange to avoid sounding too forceful or direct. Modal verbs and adverbs that express degrees of possibility can also be used in this way.

- It's <u>sort of</u> like a dull ache below my knee.
- All of this <u>stuff</u> needs to be cleared out of the room.
- Do you <u>by any chance</u> have that book I lent you last month?
- Come over at 9<u>-ish or thereabouts if you like</u>.
- We <u>should probably</u> be getting back soon.

Teaching about the differences between spoken and written language

USING TALK TO COMMUNICATE EFFECTIVELY

Talk is, arguably, our prime means of communication, and most of us do it without giving it too much thought. However, if we want our pupils to develop into really effective communicators, it's worth setting aside regular and dedicated time for this, particularly during the early secondary years.

When setting up paired or small group work, make sure that the task is purposeful and involves the need for genuine collaboration. (It can be hard to collaborate when there's no real need to.)

If you want to go further, you could set up a small research project so that pupils can reflect on the way they use talk in the classroom. You might record and transcribe their talk and ask them to evaluate the way – for example – they take turns in discussion, collaborate to negotiate an outcome, or sensitively draw in and involve less confident pupils. This might be a particularly helpful approach if you have pupils who don't readily contribute to discussion, who drift off task, or who tend to dominate at the expense of others.

RE-CREATING AUTHENTIC SPEECH IN WRITING

Dialogue in play scripts and fictional prose is not the same as a transcript of spoken language. However, you can show pupils how to draw on some of the features of spoken language to create authentic-sounding dialogue in their own writing – for example, to convey character, establish mood, and advance the action. You might draw attention to features of spoken language when you're studying a play in English literature, analysing character in a novel, or creating dialogue in narrative writing.

Use drama and role play to provide opportunities for pupils to try out spoken dialogue in less familiar contexts, perhaps taking on the role of another character so that they feel less exposed. Ask other pupils to evaluate how convincing the dialogue sounded, and make suggestions to make it more realistic.

USING SPOKEN STANDARD ENGLISH IN FORMAL SPEECH

Give pupils opportunities to use spoken Standard English in a formal debate or presentation. Alternatively, you could use role play – for example, making a case to the school governors for some new equipment, or putting a character from a novel on trial.

Formal talk can be modelled too, with oral sentence starters to support pupils as they try out less familiar language. Give pupils time to plan and prepare, and show them how to make brief speaker's notes as a self-help set of prompts.

Ask pupils to discuss whether spoken Standard English or a non-Standard form may be more appropriate in a range of situations. For example:

- A live football commentary
- A *Match of the Day*-style review of the week's football coverage with celebrity pundits
- A sports slot on a national television news channel
- A catch up with friends at school after the weekend's big match
- A press conference announcement of the new England manager by the Football Association

Ask pupils to explain how the purpose and audience affected their decision in each case.

What you need to know about writing in an informal register

When we use an informal register in writing, we can use some of the characteristics of spoken language to establish a more intimate relationship with our reader. We might also make some use of first and second person pronouns to create a chatty, almost conversational tone (We always went to my grandmother's farm for the holidays . . . You know that feeling when you just don't want to get out of bed in the morning . . .).

Features typical of an informal register include the following:

Feature	Examples
Contracted forms and abbreviations	<u>We'll</u> head off in a moment. You must take loads of <u>photos</u> when <u>you're</u> on holiday.
Question tags	This is great, <u>isn't it</u>? You did see that, <u>didn't you</u>?
Discourse markers commonly used in spoken language	Well . . . Right . . . Anyway . . . Okay . . .
Ellipsis	So much to tell you . . . Got to go now!
Multi-word verbs (phrasal and prepositional verbs)	Work out (rather than 'calculate') Come up with (rather than 'devise') Ask for (rather than 'request')
Passives using the verb 'get'	The warehouse <u>got burgled</u> last night. Our team always <u>gets beaten</u> when they're away. I <u>got</u> my hair <u>cut</u> last week.
Vague (or imprecise) vocabulary	That's such a <u>nice thing</u> to say. Is this the <u>sort of stuff</u> you wanted?
Vernacular language, including slang and idioms	The <u>kids</u> always <u>got into scrapes</u> when they were little. I was absolutely <u>knackered</u>.

Teaching about writing in an informal register

An informal register is likely to be appropriate in a range of spoken and written contexts, such as a diary, autobiography or blog, or a personal email or letter. Any attempt to recreate realistic dialogue, such as in a short story or play script, is also likely to require an informal style.

For the most part, pupils tend to know intuitively how to use an informal style: it's their default model, used in most social interactions with friends and family at home and – to a large extent – at school. However, it's still important to unpick some of the features that help us to write in an informal style so that we can do so consciously when we need to. It's important too not to treat informal writing as inferior to formal writing, but to focus firmly on its appropriateness to audience and purpose.

You could explore levels of formality and informality with pupils by giving them a set of words or phrases that have the same basic meaning. Then ask them to rank them according to their degree of formality. They could do this on a scale of 1–10 (with 1 being 'very informal' and 10 being 'very formal'), or they could simply put them in order of formality. This is best done in pairs or small groups to facilitate discussion about their decisions. Ask them to discuss appropriate contexts for each example.

May I have the butter?
Let me have the butter when you've finished with it, will you?
Some butter, please?
I'd like a little butter, if you please.
Can I get the butter? Thanks.
Would you pass the butter, please?

Alternatively, you might explore the way deliberately vague language, including modal verbs and adverbs of modality, can be used to soften an exchange when you don't want to sound too abrupt or assertive. It's not uncommon to use this type of language in emails in order to create a more friendly, familiar tone. For example:

> Hi Jean
>
> Just to let you know that I'm probably going to be arriving at around 6-ish. Hopefully this should be OK if we start the meeting straightaway. Have you had a chance to look through the papers I sent over yesterday? If not, perhaps you could have a quick look before I arrive . . .
>
> Many thanks
>
> Sue

What you need to know about writing in a formal register

Standard English is likely to be appropriate in most formal writing, but there are other features that are typically found in very formal writing:

Feature	Examples
Appropriate choice of some modal verbs in specific contexts	<u>May</u> I have another piece of cake? <u>Might</u> I ask why this is not allowed? I <u>should</u> like to offer my sincere condolences.
Lexical verbs rather than multi-word (phrasal/ prepositional) verbs	Discover (rather than 'find out') Reprimand (rather than 'tell off') Anticipate (rather than 'look forward to')
Expanded (rather than contracted) verb forms	I <u>should have</u> said something. I <u>do not</u> wish to discuss this further.
Agentless passives, especially with the dummy subject 'it'	It could <u>be argued</u> that Macbeth brought about his own downfall. It <u>is considered</u> impolite to talk while eating. It <u>is</u> generally <u>believed</u> that interest rates will rise this year.
Nominalisation	The <u>departure</u> of the guests caused much <u>concern</u>. The <u>achievement</u> of the school's netball team is a <u>cause</u> for <u>celebration</u>.
The personal pronoun 'one'	<u>One</u> might have expected better service in this restaurant. <u>One</u> can only hope that <u>one's</u> wishes will be respected.
The subjunctive	The club's owner has stipulated that the manager <u>resign</u>. I suggest that she <u>leave</u> at once. It is essential that they <u>be</u> completely satisfied.
Avoidance of preposition stranding	For whom are you looking? (rather than 'Who are you looking for?') To which pupils are you referring? (rather than 'Which pupils are you referring to?')
Inversion of wording (replacing the conjunction 'if') in some conditional clauses	<u>Had I seen</u> her, I would have said something. (rather than '<u>If I'd seen</u> her, I'd have . . .') <u>Should you accept</u> this position, we'd be delighted. (rather than '<u>If you'd accept</u> this position . . .')
Precise, often subject/ context-specific vocabulary choices	Summit (rather than 'top') Territory (rather than 'land') Predator (rather than 'hunter')

Teaching about writing in a formal register

Pupils may well have more limited exposure to formal writing and fewer opportunities to use it, so the encounters and experiences you provide at school are hugely important. It's easy to assume that pupils can simply recognise when some writing sounds more formal than other writing – while this may, to some extent, be true, it's important to teach the type of vocabulary and grammatical features that enable us to adopt a more formal style. As pupils move through key stages 3 and 4, the need to write for more formal contexts, including for examiners, will become ever more important.

Ask pupils to consider why some writing, such as a letter of application or complaint, is likely to require a relatively formal style. Then consider other writing where the writer's relationship with the reader needs to be objective, polite or authoritative, such as reports, formal argument or evaluation.

You could give pupils a handful of short texts written for different audiences, ranging from the very informal to the very formal. Ask them to rank them according to their level of formality, and identify the features that mark them out as being particularly formal. Alternatively, ask pupils to rewrite an informal piece of writing in a more formal style, drawing out the features that make each piece either formal or informal.

More informal	More formal
Here's your money back. Really sorry about all the bother. We'll get on to the manufacturers and let you know what they have to say . . .	We are pleased to enclose a cheque for £25.99 as reimbursement for your faulty goods. Please accept our apologies for the inconvenience caused by the . . .

You might share a piece of relatively formal writing, such as a letter of application, and include one or two informal features. Ask pupils to identify those that seem inappropriate for a formal context. Most importantly, ask them to explain why, and then ask them to suggest more appropriate wording.

When it comes to teaching pupils how to write in a formal style, modelling is likely to be one of the best approaches. The sequence for teaching writing can be used as follows:

- Share good models and explore their features and conventions.
- Actively demonstrate the writing process, thinking aloud as you compose.
- Invite pupils to share the composition with you, sifting and evaluating their responses.
- Support first attempts (for example, through guided group work or scaffolding).
- Provide choices for independent application.

Chapter 5
Grammar for reading and writing

What you need to know about grammar for reading and writing

This chapter addresses the grammar of the whole text, including vocabulary choices; grammatical features within sentences; and structural and cohesive devices that enable the text to 'hang together' as a whole.

There's a clear emphasis in the secondary curriculum on the application of pupils' grammatical knowledge:

- as readers – analysing and evaluating the effect of a writer's choices; and

- as writers – explicitly deploying language features to achieve particular effects on the reader.

This 'reading into writing' approach is well established. It's also well supported by research; for example, in *Getting Going: Generating, Shaping and Developing Ideas in Writing*, Professor Richard Andrews writes about the reciprocal relationship between reading (primarily a skill of language reception since the material is given) and writing (a skill of language production).

We know that reading informs writing: it builds linguistic repertoire, enabling writers to internalise the patterns, rhythms and structures of language, trying them on for size before adapting and importing them into their own writing. Good readers are often good writers, but this doesn't necessarily follow: sometimes, as readers, we need to really unpick the way a writer constructs text in order to apply this understanding in our own writing. We might think of this 'creative imitation' approach as an apprentice model, as it enables pupils to borrow from reading and learn from more experienced writers.

Although we sometimes refer to different 'text types', such as explanation or persuasion, it's important to remember that texts – especially non-fiction texts – are more typically hybrids, fulfilling multiple functions according to their intended reader and purpose. On the following pages, we'll look at a range of written texts that fulfil the following purposes:

- provide advice, instruction and explanation

- recount events, providing commentary and personal reflection

- motivate, inspire and persuade

- give an opinion, argue a case or debate a point of view

- tell a story, evoke setting and atmosphere, and convey character

In each double page spread, we'll explore an authentic, published text, focusing on the way it works in relation to its purpose, audience, form and context. Then we'll look at ways of linking this knowledge to pupils' own writing.

The following sequence for teaching writing has been used by teachers for some years now, but it's worth revisiting here because it's firmly rooted in the 'reading into writing' model. The sequence involves 'reading as a writer' through close exploration of text, unpicking the way a writer uses language to create particular effects, and then 'writing as a reader' to consciously use those features in new writing.

A sequence for teaching writing		
STAGE 1	Provide an example(s), explore its features and define the conventions.	This is where you select (or prepare) an engaging example of a text that provides a good model of the sort of writing and 'writerly' techniques you'll be teaching.
		Tease out the writer's choices and techniques and their impact on the reader, perhaps by annotating the text, and record them for future use, e.g. on a flip chart, or in pupils' writing journals if they have them.
STAGE 2	Demonstrate how a text is written and invite the class to share the composition process with you.	This is where you model the writing process, demonstrating 'writerly' behaviours, such as rehearsing sentences orally, re-reading and editing.
		Think aloud as you write, deliberating on – and explaining – your language choices. When you judge it to be appropriate, draw pupils in to share the composition with you, prompting, sifting, evaluating and challenging contributions from the class.
STAGE 3	Scaffold first attempts and support independent writing.	This is where you support pupils as they apply what they've learnt to become independent writers.
		Depending on pupils' particular needs, you might offer sentence starters or a writing frame, display key features and conventions, or provide the content so that pupils have less cognitive load to bear. You might ask pupils to work with a writing partner, or you might lead a guided writing group.
		Importantly, you'll want to encourage pupils to deploy and adapt the features, conventions and strategies that you've explored together.

KNOWLEDGE

Grammar for reading and writing

What you need to know about writing that provides advice, instruction and explanation

To be fair, this type of writing is not likely to be the sole remit of the English Department. Much explanatory writing is likely to be found across the curriculum, in subjects such as science, history or technology. What's more, pupils will encounter instructional writing well beyond the school curriculum – just think about instruction manuals, recipes and self-help books.

READING AS A WRITER

There are a number of really interesting features in the text on the opposite page: 'Wildflowers for bees: how to attract bees to your garden', published on the website of the Woodland Trust.

In terms of its overall structure, the concise introduction immediately states the issue – that wild bees and other pollinators are in decline – and then swiftly moves on to reassure the reader that there are ways of reversing this trend. The reader is able to navigate the text via a sequence of five numbered tips for attracting bees to the garden, with each tip taking the form of a brief but clear instruction followed up by further elaboration and explanatory detail.

Thematic linkage makes the text cohesive (*Wild bees . . . pollinators . . . bee-friendly . . . bumble-bee species . . . buzzing . . . native insects . . . rarer bees . . . solitary bees and insects . . . honeybees*). Although the five numbered tips are free-standing, each works with the others to provide the reader with a cumulative list of actions that can be taken for maximum impact.

As you'd expect in writing that tells the reader how to do something, the imperative form is used throughout (*Aim for a good variety . . . avoid plants . . . Choose winter . . . Read the label and avoid using . . . Create insect houses*). However, in order to avoid the rather peremptory manner of the command form, the tone is frequently softened through the use of vague language (*In general, avoid . . .*) and contracted forms (*If you can't bear to let your lawn grow, consider . . . Don't use . . .*). Similarly, the use of declaratives, using modal verbs with the second person 'you' (*there are things you can do . . . you should be able to entice . . . You can make . . . or you can buy*), creates the effect of friendly and informed advice freely offered.

Interestingly, the opening two paragraphs consist of declaratives with not a single command in sight. They provide information – a statement of the problem followed immediately by reassuring information – predominantly through the use of verbs and adverbs of modality (*should be able to . . . and possibly even . . . will ensure your plants . . .*) – offering encouraging degrees of certainty.

Vocabulary choices are largely subject-specific (*pollinators . . . nectar . . . evolved . . . neonicotinoids . . .*) and include scientific names (*Bombus hortorum*), showing that the writer really knows her stuff. However, these are set alongside more informal vocabulary choices (*getting your garden buzzing . . . tips . . . great for bees . . .*), creating a friendly, conversational tone.

Although its prime purpose as a 'how to' text is to explain, this piece is also highly informative, adding fuel to our earlier point that texts rarely do just one thing, but are essentially hybrids.

WRITING AS A READER

Once you've explored the text with pupils, follow stages 2 and 3 of the teaching sequence, modelling and scaffolding another 'how to' text. Then ask pupils to use some of the features and techniques in a 'how to' text of their own choice: for example, how to create a hedgehog-friendly garden; how to stay safe on the beach; or how to train a dragon!

WILDFLOWERS FOR BEES: HOW TO ATTRACT BEES TO YOUR GARDEN

Wild bees and other pollinators are in decline. But there are things you can do in your garden to help reverse this trend by making your garden bee-friendly.

Wherever you live in the UK, you should be able to entice around six bumblebee species to your garden, and possibly even ten. In return for getting your garden buzzing, pollinators will ensure your plants continue to reproduce through seed and that many fruit and vegetable crops such as apples, strawberries and tomatoes successfully set fruit.

Five tips for attracting bees to your garden

1   Create diverse plantings

Aim for a good variety of pollen rich flowers that have different flower shapes and a range of flowering periods from early spring to late summer and even throughout the winter if you can.

Bumblebee species have different length tongues that are adapted to feed from different shaped flowers. For example the longest tongued species, *Bombus hortorum*, prefers deep flowers such as honeysuckle and foxglove.

In general, avoid plants with double or multi-petalled flowers. Their flowers are filled with petals and pollinators find them difficult to access. The flowers also often lack nectar and pollen.

2   Plant wildflowers and native species

Native plants have evolved alongside our native insects and some of our rarer bees tend to favour native wildflowers. There are other benefits to wildflowers too. They are often easy to grow and thrive in the average garden, being hardy and much more resistant to slugs and mildew than other garden flowers.

Some trees and shrubs are also great for bees as they provide masses of flowers in one place. Choose winter and early spring flowering trees such as apple, wild cherry, willow and hazel.

3   Don't use pesticides

Garden chemicals containing neonicotinoids (thiacloprid and acetamiprid) are still approved as an insecticide for home and garden use and are available today at most garden centres and DIY shops. Read the label and avoid using them.

4   Make a bee house

Create insect houses in to your garden to provide nesting sites for solitary bees and insects. Different bee species require different habitats.

You can make your own simple bee house or you can buy a commercially made bee house. Fix bee boxes in a south-facing spot but not in direct sunlight. Also make sure the entrance points downwards so that rain doesn't get in.

5   Retain lawn weeds

Lawn weeds such as dandelions are excellent bee plants, providing vital pollen early in the season. White clover attracts masses of honeybees, while the longer tongued bumblebees prefer red clover. If you can't bear to let your lawn grow, consider leaving a patch that's less frequently mown to give them a chance to flower.

By Helen Keating © The Woodland Trust 2017

What you need to know about writing that recounts events, providing commentary and personal reflection

There's a wide range of writing that might involve a recount of real or imagined events: biographical or autobiographical writing, such as memoirs and travel writing; reportage, including news reports, journalistic articles, eye-witness accounts and sports reports; and reviews that incorporate some element of evaluative judgement.

There are plenty of opportunities for pupils to use this type of writing in English literature (reviewing a theatre production or retelling part of a novel from a different perspective) or in other subjects such as history or geography.

READING AS A WRITER

The text on the opposite page is an extract from Sir Ernest Shackleton's biographical account of his Antarctic expedition in 1914–17. In this extract, he recounts the loss of his ship, the *Endurance*, which broke up in pack ice.

Shackleton's first-person account of the events vividly recreates the scene. Past tense verbs (*split . . . tore*) including the past progressive (*was increasing . . . were breaking . . . was pouring . . . were simply annihilating*) portray the destructive force of the ice, enabling the reader to witness alongside him the unfolding events.

Although the narrator tells us he 'cannot describe the impression of relentless destruction', this is precisely what he does. Just look at the expanded noun phrases, some of which use –ing verbs as adjectives (*the <u>driving</u> floe . . . The <u>twisting</u>, <u>grinding</u> floes . . . the <u>quivering</u> deck . . . the force of millions of tons of <u>moving</u> ice*), while others incorporate non-finite –ing verbs and preposition phrases (*the great beams <u>bending</u> and then <u>snapping with a noise like heavy gunfire</u>*) to add descriptive detail.

The apt use of the passive voice (*The ship was hove stern up by the pressure . . . the impression of relentless destruction that was forced upon me*) contrasts with the active voice used elsewhere in the piece, presenting the ship and crew as helpless victims of the formidable ice floe.

As with most recounts, events are presented chronologically. The parenthetical information in the opening sentence (*our last on the ship*) establishes the significance of this particular morning. Extensive use of co-ordinated clauses, linked by the conjunction 'and', slows the pace, while adverbs (*steadily . . . laterally . . . upwards . . . below . . . sideways . . . down . . . around*) evoke the relentless movement as the ship is crushed. Conjunctions and adverbials of time (*This morning . . . at 4 P.M. . . . Then . . . Again . . . at 5 P.M. . . . Just before leaving . . . as*) move events to their inevitable conclusion, with the solitary narrator bearing witness to his final moments on the ship.

WRITING AS A READER

Once you've explored this and other recount texts with pupils, follow stages 2 and 3 of the teaching sequence, modelling and scaffolding another piece of recount writing. Then ask pupils to use some of the features and techniques in a recount of their choice. You might give them a suggested opening: What should have been just another day at school turned into the worst/ best/ funniest/ saddest/ most memorable day of my life.

This morning, our last on the ship, the weather was clear, with a gentle south-southeasterly to south-southwesterly breeze. From the crow's nest there was no sign of land of any sort. The pressure was increasing steadily, and the passing hours brought no relief or respite for the ship. The attack of the ice reached its climax at 4 P.M. The ship was hove stern up by the pressure, and the driving floe, moving laterally across the stern, split the rudder and tore out the rudder post and stern post. Then, while we watched, the ice loosened and the *Endurance* sank a little. The decks were breaking upwards and the water was pouring in below. Again the pressure began, and at 5 P.M. I ordered all hands on to the ice. The twisting, grinding floes were working their will at last on the ship. It was a sickening sensation to feel the decks breaking up under one's feet, the great beams bending and then snapping with a noise like heavy gunfire. The water was overmastering the pumps, and to avoid an explosion when it reached the boilers I had to give orders for the fires to be drawn and the steam let down. The plans for abandoning the ship in case of emergency had been made well in advance, and men and dogs descended to the floe and made their way to the comparative safety of an unbroken portion of the floe without a hitch. Just before leaving, I looked down the engine room skylight as I stood on the quivering deck, and saw the engines dropping sideways as the stays and bed plates gave way. I cannot describe the impression of relentless destruction that was forced upon me as I looked down and around. The floes, with the force of millions of tons of moving ice behind them, were simply annihilating the ship.

From 'South: The *Endurance* Expedition' by Ernest Shackleton

What you need to know about writing that motivates, inspires and persuades

Political rhetoric and campaign literature are part of our everyday lives, as is promotional material such as leaflets and advertisements. In English lessons, we're also likely to study speeches and polemical poetry.

It's hugely important for readers and listeners to know not only when they're being influenced by what they're reading or hearing, but also how a text – be it written or spoken – actually creates this effect. That way, they can deploy similar conventions themselves in talk and in writing. If we want our pupils to be discriminating readers and assured writers, we need to teach them how language can manipulate and persuade, inspire and motivate.

READING AS A WRITER

The text on the opposite page, 'Adopt a turtle', published on the website of the WWF, is part of the organisation's work to protect some of the planet's iconic animals. As such, it seeks to inform, inspire and motivate, persuading the reader to take action by adopting an animal.

The text is easy to navigate: there's a heading, sub-headings and lists, including bullet points at the end which help the reader to see 'at a glance' how their support will make a difference. The overall structure steers the reader from the opening section, with its startling facts about turtles, to the encouraging news about the impact of animal adoptions, and further information detailing specific threats to the turtle population. The text concludes with positive examples of the WWF's current work and ways in which the reader's support will enable it to develop.

Thematic linkage (*extinction . . . threats . . . destruction . . . poached . . . raided . . . damage . . . destroy*) makes the text cohesive, as do pronouns (*Animal adoptions . . . They not only help . . . Climate change is causing sea levels to rise, and increase the number, and the intensity, of storms. This can damage . . . to help protect those beaches and the turtles that use them*).

The present tense creates a sense of immediacy, and the present progressive form in particular (*is destroying . . . we're identifying important nesting sites and working with . . .*) heightens the sense of urgency, showing the reader what's actually happening as they're reading. Use of the first and second person (*yours . . . our . . . We're . . . Your . . . us*) forges a direct connection between writer and reader.

Vocabulary choices also play their part: adjectives (*huge boost . . . vital work*) and adverbs (*hundreds, even thousands . . . amazingly*) intensify the importance of the challenge, while verbs with emotive connotations (*adopt . . . raided*) appeal to the reader's protective instinct.

While the prime purpose of this text is to persuade the reader to adopt an animal, the piece is also highly informative, filling the reader with a sense of wonder at the lives of these amazing creatures as well as a desire to help them.

WRITING AS A READER

Once you've explored the text with pupils, follow stages 2 and 3 of the teaching sequence, modelling and scaffolding another persuasive text. Then ask pupils to use some of the features and techniques in a persuasive text of their own choice: for example, a campaign leaflet from an animal charity, a magazine 'advertorial' (written to look like an article but funded by the advertiser), or a website from a pressure group.

ADOPT A TURTLE

It's estimated that only around 1 in 1,000 turtle hatchlings make it to adulthood.

There are seven species – hawksbill, leatherback, loggerhead, flatback, olive ridley, Kemp's ridley and green turtle – and at least six of the seven species are at risk of extinction.

YOUR ADOPTION REALLY HELPS

Animal adoptions like yours give a huge boost to our work. They not only help fund projects to work with local communities to monitor turtle movements and protect their habitat but also fund our other vital work around the world.

Marine turtles are excellent navigators – they often migrate hundreds, even thousands of kilometres between feeding and nesting grounds. Male turtles never leave the sea, but females come ashore to lay eggs – amazingly to the same beach where they themselves hatched.

THREATS

FISHING	HABITAT DESTRUCTION	POACHING	CLIMATE CHANGE
Marine turtles need to get to the surface to breathe, and if they get caught up in fishing gear, they can drown.	One of the main threats turtles face is the destruction of their habitats. Development along coastlines is destroying nesting beaches, making it impossible for female turtles to lay their eggs.	Turtles are poached for their meat and shells, and nests are raided for eggs, which are seen as a delicacy in some cultures.	Climate change is causing sea levels to rise, and increase the number, and the intensity, of storms. This can damage and destroy nesting beaches.

HOW WE CAN HELP

We're reducing the negative impact of fishing practices on marine turtles by promoting the use of less-harmful fishing gear – for example, 'circle hooks' instead of traditional 'j' hooks can reduce accidental capture of turtles by up to 80%.

We're helping protect marine turtle habitats. For example, along the coast of east Africa we're identifying important nesting sites and working with local people to help protect those beaches and the turtles that use them.

Your adoption and support will help us:

✓ reduce illegal fishing
✓ promote sustainable fishing practices
✓ expand and create marine protected areas
✓ help local communities conserve and manage their natural resources
✓ help strengthen law enforcement to halt the illegal trade in turtles

Source: WWF-UK

What you need to know about writing that gives an opinion, argues a case or debates a point of view

Discursive writing (or balanced argument) in which two sides of an argument are debated is a well-established form of writing in English lessons, but it's also important to teach pupils how to construct a formal argument – such as a newspaper editorial – that expresses a single point of view.

Some of the features of persuasive writing – such as rhetorical questions, direct address to the reader and the 'pattern of three' – are often employed in formal argument. However, whereas persuasive writing typically urges the reader to actually do something, formal argument tends to be more interested in shifting opinion.

READING AS A WRITER

The text on the opposite page is an article written by sociologist Frank Furedi, and was first published in an online magazine. Notice how there's nothing ambiguous about its title: the piece sets out its stall from the start and argues its case right the way through to its unequivocal conclusion.

Counter-evidence is cited and then immediately challenged (*The Sunday Times has reported that . . . However, recent press reports have tended to misinterpret . . . According to a National Union of Students [NUS] survey . . . If this were true . . . Young people today are said to be . . . But can anyone seriously claim that . . .*).

Cohesion is achieved in a number of ways: adverbs of logic (*However . . . Therefore*) challenge received opinion; subordinating conjunctions and adverbials (*In turn . . . When children are treated . . . by the time young people . . . Once exam stress is . . . Until the medicalisation . . .*) propel the argument forwards; and pronouns (*If this were true . . . But clearly, it isn't . . . This happens to young people . . . This is particularly striking*) refer backwards, supporting connections across the text.

Adverbs of stance (*But clearly, it isn't . . . Unfortunately, medicalising children . . .*) and telling choices of vocabulary (*this so-called mental-health crisis*) make clear the writer's position, as does the brief transition to the first person (*When I went . . . we did not . . . to describe our feelings*) – an interesting feature in an otherwise relatively impersonal piece.

Expanded noun phrases and nominalisation add weight and gravitas to the writing (*the demand for differential treatment at exam time . . . the traditional boundary between health and illness . . . the pathologisation of children's behaviour . . . a wider process of medicalisation in the classroom*) and heighten the impact of the short, single clause sentence (*But clearly, it isn't*).

We could, of course, also point out the rhetorical question (*But can anyone . . . pressure-free lives?*) and the pattern of three (*words like stress, trauma or depression*).

WRITING AS A READER

Once you've explored this and other opinion pieces with pupils, follow stages 2 and 3 of the teaching sequence, modelling and scaffolding another formal argument text. Then ask pupils to use some of the features and techniques in a formal argument of their own. It's important that you give them choice here – they'll produce a stronger argument if they're writing about something they know and feel passionately about, be it through personal experience or research.

EXAM STRESS IS NOT A MENTAL ILLNESS

The Sunday Times has reported that the University of Cambridge approved requests for 218 students to have alternative exam arrangements last year – triple the amount of students allowed special measures five years ago.

However, recent press reports have tended to misinterpret the nature of this problem. They accept the premise that the demand for differential treatment at exam time is the outcome of a mental-health crisis currently sweeping campuses. They rarely pause and ponder what constitutes a mental-health issue, and whether these claims are serious.

According to a National Union of Students (NUS) survey in 2015, 78 per cent of undergraduates suffered from mental-health issues during the previous year. If this were true, being mentally ill would be the norm on campus. But clearly, it isn't. Instead, the traditional boundary between health and illness has become corroded due to society's inclination to interpret the problems of life through the prism of mental health.

This happens to young people at an early age. One of the most disturbing developments in recent times is the pathologisation of children's behaviour. This is particularly striking in education, where the normal tensions and insecurities of childhood are often discussed in terms of medical diagnoses. The invention of conditions such as 'schoolphobia' and 'test anxiety' reflects a wider process of medicalisation in the classroom.

Dramatic, headline-grabbing figures regarding an epidemic of exam-related stress in schools accompany claims that children are under unprecedented pressure, due to the proliferation of testing and the burden of schoolwork. In turn, children often voice their concerns about school life through a psychological vocabulary. When I went to primary school, we did not use words like stress, trauma or depression to describe our feelings.

Unfortunately, medicalising children can become a self-fulfilling prophecy. When children are treated as potential patients they may well be inclined to accept the role assigned to them. Therefore it's not surprising that by the time young people arrive at university they experience the challenges they face as mental-health issues. Once exam stress is medicalised this new 'condition' can only spread.

Young people today are said to be subject to unprecedented pressures, whether it's an unreasonable regime of testing in schools or the financial insecurity and poverty of being at university. No doubt, students face pressure. But can anyone seriously claim that previous generations of young people led pressure-free lives? Until the medicalisation of young people is challenged, this so-called mental-health crisis will get worse and worse.

Professor Frank Furedi: Exam stress is not a mental illness (*spiked online*)

What you need to know about writing that tells a story, evokes setting and atmosphere, and conveys character

We're mostly looking at narrative fiction here – novels and short stories – although much of the poetry your pupils will be studying is likely to be highly descriptive and may well incorporate elements of narrative too. It's the staple foodstuff of the English Department.

READING AS A WRITER

The text on the opposite page is an extract from *Great Expectations* by Charles Dickens, published in 1860–61. In this extract, the young Pip visits Miss Havisham.

The extract is framed by dialogue – at the start, by Miss Havisham's peremptory command which sends Pip to wait for her in the room; and towards the end, by her somewhat morbid pronouncement about the bridal table. These snippets of one-sided dialogue advance the action by locating Pip in the room, and also convey character – not least through Pip's silent obedience, wry misgivings and adverse reaction to Miss Havisham's physical presence.

Pronouns (. . . *the chamber . . .* <u>*It*</u> *was spacious . . . An epergne or centre-piece of some kind . . .* <u>*it*</u> *was . . .*) and synonymous references (*a long table with a tablecloth spread on it . . . the yellow expanse . . . the long table . . . the table . . .* and *speckled-legged spiders . . . black-beetles . . . These crawling things*) support cohesion.

Like much Victorian literature, the sentences tend to be long with multiple clauses: here they are typically controlled through co-ordinating conjunctions (*and, or, but*) and semi-colons. Extensive use of the complex subordinator 'as if' invites comparison, enabling the reader to comprehend the scene. The final sentence, with its layers of fronted subordination, is all the more powerful for the way it withholds the main clause (*I shrank under her touch*) until the very end.

Details are positioned for effect: the centrality of the bridal table (*The most prominent object*) with its spider-infested centre-piece, and the communities of creatures – some seen, others heard – that so fascinate the young narrator. Expanded noun phrases (*an airless smell that was oppressive . . . the reluctant smoke which hung in the room . . . Certain wintry branches of candles on the high chimney-piece . . . speckled-legged spiders with blotchy bodies . . . some circumstance of the greatest public importance . . . These crawling things*) and verbs modified by adverbs (*completely excluded . . . lately kindled . . . faintly lighted . . . faintly troubled . . . so heavily overhung . . . groped about*) and preposition phrases (*covered* <u>*with dust and mould*</u> *. . . overhung* <u>*with cobwebs*</u> *. . . rattling* <u>*behind the panels*</u>) add a density to the detailed description of the room, creating images that seem to pile up, transfixing the reader so that we are as startled as Pip by Miss Havisham's sudden reappearance.

WRITING AS A READER

Once you've explored this and more modern narrative fiction with pupils, follow stages 2 and 3 of the teaching sequence, modelling and scaffolding a section of descriptive narrative. Then ask pupils to use some of the features and techniques in a narrative of their choice. Alternatively, you might ask them to write in the style of an author – for example, an additional chapter or a section written from the perspective of another character.

'Then go into that opposite room,' said she, pointing at the door behind me with her withered hand, 'and wait there till I come.'

I crossed the staircase landing, and entered the room she indicated. From that room, too, the daylight was completely excluded, and it had an airless smell that was oppressive. A fire had been lately kindled in the damp old-fashioned grate, and it was more disposed to go out than to burn up, and the reluctant smoke which hung in the room seemed colder than the clearer air – like our own marsh mist. Certain wintry branches of candles on the high chimney-piece faintly lighted the chamber: or, it would be more expressive to say, faintly troubled its darkness. It was spacious, and I dare say had once been handsome, but every discernible thing in it was covered with dust and mould, and dropping to pieces. The most prominent object was a long table with a tablecloth spread on it, as if a feast had been in preparation when the house and the clocks all stopped together. An epergne or centre-piece of some kind was in the middle of this cloth; it was so heavily overhung with cobwebs that its form was quite indistinguishable; and, as I looked along the yellow expanse out of which I remember its seeming to grow, like a black fungus, I saw speckled-legged spiders with blotchy bodies running home to it, and running out from it, as if some circumstance of the greatest public importance had just transpired in the spider community.

I heard the mice too, rattling behind the panels, as if the same occurrence were important to their interests. But, the black-beetles took no notice of the agitation, and groped about the hearth in a ponderous elderly way, as if they were short-sighted and hard of hearing, and not on terms with one another.

These crawling things had fascinated my attention and I was watching them from a distance, when Miss Havisham laid a hand upon my shoulder. In her other hand she had a crutch-headed stick on which she leaned, and she looked like the Witch of the place.

'This,' said she, pointing to the long table with her stick, 'is where I will be laid when I am dead. They shall come and look at me here.'

With some vague misgiving that she might get upon the table then and there and die at once, the complete realisation of the ghastly waxwork at the Fair, I shrank under her touch.

From *Great Expectations* by Charles Dickens

Chapter 6
Writing about language use

What you need to know about writing about language use

The previous chapter focused on 'reading as a writer' and 'writing as a reader' – in other words, analysing the features of a text that make it effective and then drawing on those features and conventions in writing – an apprentice model that borrows from reading.

This chapter is different. Like the previous chapter, its starting point is the analysis of text; unlike the previous chapter, its focus then shifts from writing in a similar style to the analysed text, to writing <u>about</u> it, critically evaluating it in terms of its structure, grammar and vocabulary choices.

Most English teachers are comfortable with literary terminology and figurative language: many of us cut our teeth on this as students ourselves, analysing text and subtext and relishing the intellectual satisfaction of the process.

But this chapter delves further into the way we can explore the grammar of a text, helping our pupils to use linguistic terminology precisely and with confidence.

Of course, it can be frustrating when pupils don't share our pleasure of textual analysis, or lose interest quickly.

But if we use the 'reading into writing' approach in the previous chapter, and establish it from the early secondary years, pupils will be used to approaching texts as writers. They'll be used to thinking about text as something a writer has crafted, using particular features and techniques appropriate to its intended purpose and reader. In other words, they'll have been active participants rather than passive recipients.

That said, many pupils do find it hard to get started, to know what to write or what kind of language to use. They may lack the confidence to analyse a text and comment on the language used. Terms like 'language features' and 'technique' can seem vague and somewhat daunting if pupils don't know what to look for.

There are, however, things you can do to help:

1. When discussing a text, model the kind of language – including the terminology – that you expect pupils to use.

2. Use the sequence for teaching writing in the previous chapter to teach pupils how to write in the style of the formal expository essay, modelling the relatively formal, analytic language required.

3. Show pupils how to embed quotations neatly and aptly into their writing to support the points they make.

4. Teach pupils how to structure their response by sharing good examples of formal essays or examination answers.

5. Give pupils a 'toolkit' so that they know what to look for in a text. The question prompts on the opposite page can be used, although they shouldn't be seen as a straitjacket, with an answer required for every single question. Use them flexibly with pupils as a helpful framework.

In writing about language use, you'll be able to draw on much of what we've already covered in this book. And by sharing the terminology, you'll be giving pupils the language – or the metalanguage – they need to talk and write about language with economy and confidence.

Teaching pupils to write about language use: a toolkit

1. Purpose and audience

    This should always be our starting point.

    - What kind of text is this?
    - Who's it written for?
    - What's its purpose?
    - Where might we find a text like this?

    By answering these questions, we're well on our way to understanding what sort of writerly techniques the writer might have used to affect the reader's response.

2. Structure and cohesion

    - What's the main underlying principle in terms of the way the text is structured? Is it chronological or non-chronological? If it's an extract from a longer text, does the writer position details for effect to create tension or suspense?
    - How cohesive is the writing? How do conjunctions and adverbials, pronouns and determiners support cohesion? What about thematic linkage, deliberate repetition or synonymous references?
    - Is there anything interesting about the layout or typographical features, such as bullet points, sub-headings or lists?

3. Voice and viewpoint

    - What perspective is the text written from? Does it use the first, second or third person? Does the viewpoint shift? Is the reader directly addressed?
    - Is there any use of the passive voice? If so, how does this affect the way information is presented?
    - What's the level of formality and how is this achieved? Is the tone friendly, familiar and confiding or formal, distant and objective?

4. Literary and rhetorical devices

    - Is there much figurative language, or language that appeals to the senses? Is there any rhetorical language, patterning or repetition?

5. Sentences

    - Which sentence forms are used? Are they mainly declaratives? Or are interrogatives and exclamatives used? Are there any imperatives? If so, does the writer use the bare imperative, or is the tone softened, for example, by using declaratives with modal verbs as polite directives?
    - What do we notice about the clause types? Do sentences contain multiple clauses or are they short, single-clause sentences? Are co-ordinated clauses joined by co-ordinating conjunctions or by colons and semi-colons? What can we say about subordinate clauses? Are they fronted or embedded? Are there any non-finite clauses?
    - Are there any sentence 'fragments'? If so, what's the effect of these?

6. Vocabulary

    - What do we notice about the type of vocabulary used? Is it highly technical and subject-specific? Or is it colloquial and informal?
    - What do we notice about word class? (Is the writing quite dense and noun-heavy?)
    - Are words chosen for their descriptive impact? Do they carry multiple meanings that the reader has to infer? Are words chosen for their emotive impact?
    - Is there any repetition or patterning of words?

Teaching pupils to write about language use

The following passage is an extract from *Jane Eyre* by Charlotte Brontë. It describes the scene towards the end of the novel when Jane returns to Thornfield Hall only to find it destroyed by fire.

I looked with timorous joy towards a stately house: I saw a blackened ruin.

No need to cower behind a gate-post, indeed! – to peep up at chamber lattices, fearing life was astir behind them! No need to listen for doors opening – to fancy steps on the pavement or the gravel-walk! The lawn, the grounds were trodden and waste: the portal yawned void. The front was as I had once seen it in a dream, but a shell-like wall, very high and very fragile-looking, perforated with paneless windows: no roof, no battlements, no chimneys – all had crashed in.

And there was the silence of death about it: the solitude of a lonesome wild. No wonder that letters addressed to people here had never received an answer: as well despatch epistles to a vault in a church aisle. The grim blackness of the stones told by what fate the Hall had fallen – by conflagration: but how kindled? What story belonged to this disaster? What loss, besides mortar and marble and woodwork had followed upon it? Had life been wrecked as well as property? If so, whose? Dreadful question: there was no one here to answer it – not even dumb sign, mute token.

From *Jane Eyre* by Charlotte Brontë

Teaching pupils to write about language use

Let's imagine we've been asked to consider how the writer uses language to describe the effect of the scene on the narrator.

We can start by 'reading as a writer', drawing out some of the structural features, sentence grammar and vocabulary choices, perhaps by annotating a copy of the text so that pupils can understand our thought processes. This is rather like modelling writing, but instead we're modelling 'readerly' behaviours (pupils may well be familiar with this approach from guided reading at key stage 2).

Think aloud as you annotate so that pupils can see how you relate the question prompts in the 'toolkit' to the text. This is stage 1 of the sequence for teaching writing.

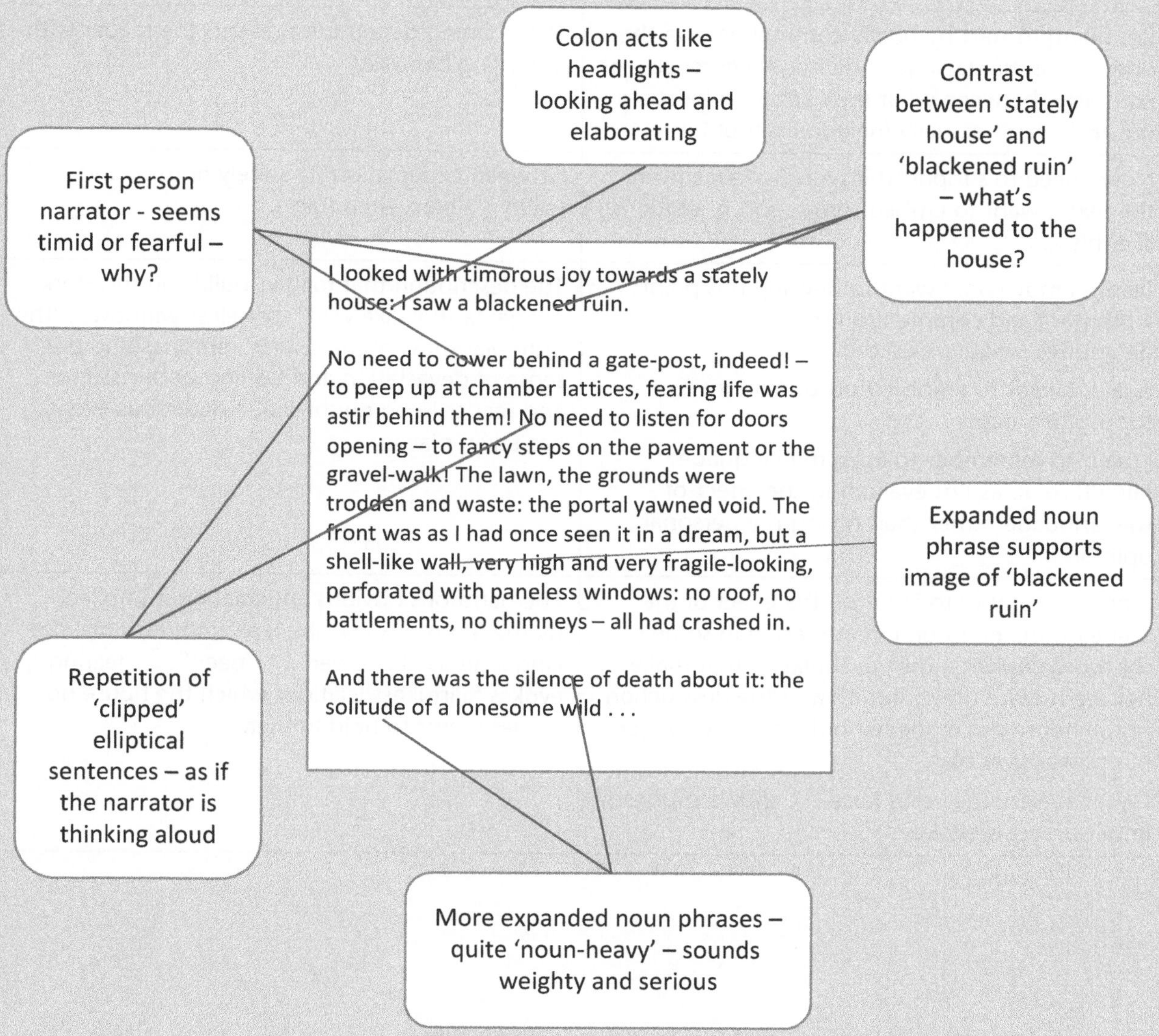

Colon acts like headlights – looking ahead and elaborating

Contrast between 'stately house' and 'blackened ruin' – what's happened to the house?

First person narrator - seems timid or fearful – why?

I looked with timorous joy towards a stately house: I saw a blackened ruin.

No need to cower behind a gate-post, indeed! – to peep up at chamber lattices, fearing life was astir behind them! No need to listen for doors opening – to fancy steps on the pavement or the gravel-walk! The lawn, the grounds were trodden and waste: the portal yawned void. The front was as I had once seen it in a dream, but a shell-like wall, very high and very fragile-looking, perforated with paneless windows: no roof, no battlements, no chimneys – all had crashed in.

And there was the silence of death about it: the solitude of a lonesome wild . . .

Expanded noun phrase supports image of 'blackened ruin'

Repetition of 'clipped' elliptical sentences – as if the narrator is thinking aloud

More expanded noun phrases – quite 'noun-heavy' – sounds weighty and serious

Figure 6.1 Text annotation

Teaching pupils to write about language use

This type of text annotation is a useful stepping stone to writing about a text in a more analytical way, so the next step is to show pupils how to expand their initial responses into more considered prose by 'writing as a reader'. This is stage 2 of the sequence for teaching writing.

Model the way you go about shaping your initial textual analysis into a formal written response before drawing pupils in to share the composition with you. At its best, modelled writing is carried out naturally and spontaneously, but many teachers like to have a semi-prepared script to use as a prompt.

Here's how it might work in practice:

You say . . .	You write . . .
I'm going to start by briefly commenting on the opening of the passage – the huge difference – or contrast – between what the narrator expects to see and what's actually there in front of her . . .	The opening paragraph presents the reader with a startling contrast
Now I need to support this with evidence from the text. I want to embed some short quotations like this . . .	between expectation ('a stately house') and reality ('a blackened ruin').
Before I move on, I want to develop this point a bit more and comment on some of the descriptive language used . . . Again, I want to embed short quotations to support my point . . . I need to remember to keep my language fairly formal, as I'm evaluating the effect of the language rather than giving my personal opinion . . .	The description that follows builds on this stark image: 'a shell-like wall', 'paneless windows', 'the grim blackness of the stones', emphasising the sense of devastation and leaving both narrator and reader in no doubt that a disastrous event has taken place.
I must remember to focus on the effect of the scene on the narrator. I'm interested in some of the word choices – the vocabulary – that make her seem quite timid. But it's as if the destruction of the house has made her bolder – it no longer has power over her . . . I want to vary the verbs I use . . . shows/suggests/implies/reveals/evokes . . .	The narrator's obvious anticipation is implied by the 'timorous joy' she feels; interestingly, the language used ('cower' . . . 'peep' . . . 'fearing'), evokes fearful associations which the house no longer seems to hold for her.

Teaching pupils to write about language use

If you're really not comfortable with this approach, you could offer pupils a ready-made example and ask them to offer suggestions for improvement, or give them an example of the type of response you want them to write and ask them to pick out the features that make it effective.

Here's how you could tease out some of the other points you might want to make:

- Vocabulary choices towards the beginning of the extract evoke the fearful feelings that the narrator seems to associate with the house (*timorous . . . cower . . . peep . . . fearing . . . fancy*), causing the reader to wonder about her earlier association with it.
- The two independent clauses separated by a colon in the brief opening paragraph present a stark contrast between what the narrator expected to see (*a stately house*) and what she actually saw (*a blackened ruin*).
- The subsequent paragraphs develop the image of *the blackened ruin*, with thematically linked details that support cohesion (*a shell-like wall . . . perforated with paneless windows . . . the grim blackness of the stones . . . this disaster . . . conflagration*).
- Textual patterning (*no roof, no battlements, no chimneys*) has the effect of slowing the pace, enabling the reader to gradually absorb the scene alongside the narrator.
- The series of questions in the third paragraph, and the elliptical sentence 'fragments' (*No need to cower . . . Dreadful question*) replicate the narrator's train of thought as she tries to make sense of what she sees.
- Expanded noun phrases, incorporating nominalisation (*the silence of death . . . the solitude of a lonesome wild . . . The grim blackness of the stones*) add a sense of solemnity to the description, leading both narrator and reader to wonder about the potential loss of life.

Then go on to scaffold pupils' first attempts as they apply what they've learnt to their own writing. You might offer sentence starters, display an annotated copy of the analysed text or work with a guided writing group. This is stage 3 of the sequence for teaching writing.

This type of 'writing about writing' is not likely to be familiar to pupils – it's not the kind of writing they typically encounter – so introduce it early and practise it 'little and often'. This should build their confidence and stamina, enabling them to produce this kind of writing independently so that writing for examinations will feel like a natural progression.

Glossary

Active voice The term 'voice' refers to the way information is presented in a clause. Writers have a choice of two voices – active or passive – but the active is the most frequently used. The active voice places the focus on the agent (or the 'doer'), as the subject of the verb and the agent are one and the same.

- Sam broke the vase. (Sam is both subject and agent.)
- The gale-force winds felled the trees. (The gale-force winds are both subject and agent.)

See 'passive voice' for passive versions of these sentences.

Adjective A word that modifies or gives more information about a noun or a pronoun. Adjectives are typically positioned directly before the noun where they are called attributive adjectives, but they can appear in other positions too.

- Dale possessed a kind of <u>hypnotic</u> charm.
- We had made a <u>late</u> start that morning.
- The weather, <u>wet</u> and <u>windy</u>, rather spoilt the day.
- The sea was <u>calm</u> last night.

Adverb A word that modifies a verb, an adjective or another adverb.

- Thomas staggered <u>slowly</u> down the icy lane. (The underlined adverb modifies the verb 'staggered'.)
- Thomas staggered slowly down the <u>treacherously</u> icy lane. (The underlined adverb modifies the adjective 'icy'.)
- Thomas staggered <u>somewhat</u> slowly down the treacherously icy lane. (The underlined adverb modifies the adverb 'slowly'.)

Adverbs can tell us about time (they are coming <u>soon</u>), frequency (I <u>rarely</u> eat chocolate), place (she used to live <u>here</u>), manner (it began to snow <u>heavily</u>) and degree (that's a <u>very</u> funny story).

Conjunctive adverbs (such as <u>however</u>, <u>therefore</u>, or <u>consequently</u>) can support cohesion in writing. Adverbs of stance (or 'disjuncts') can indicate a writer's viewpoint (<u>unfortunately</u>, I won't be able to make the meeting).

Adverbial A word, phrase or clause that functions as an adverb, typically to modify a verb or a clause. Adverbials can be single words, phrases or clauses.

- Molly pruned the roses <u>recently</u>.
- Molly pruned the roses <u>with her new secateurs</u>.
- Molly pruned the roses <u>once their blooms had faded</u>.

Affix	Affixes are attached (or affixed) to the base form of a word to change its meaning or to make a new word (<u>un</u>mistak<u>able</u>). While they carry meaning, they can't be used independently of the base word. Prefixes and suffixes are the most common affixes in English.
Agreement	Sometimes referred to as 'concord', agreement refers to the way a finite verb matches (or agrees with) its subject in terms of number and person.

- This <u>book is</u> my all-time favourite.
- Those <u>books are</u> in the sale this week.
- <u>She looks</u> like her sister.
- <u>They look</u> like each other.

This is an important issue when comparing Standard English with non-Standard varieties where lack of subject/verb agreement is typically a key feature.

Anaphoric reference	A cohesive feature in which a word (typically a pronoun) or group of words refers back to someone or something previously mentioned.

- <u>The small boy</u> began to whimper; <u>he</u> had lost sight of his mother.

Antonym	A word that has the opposite meaning to another word (hot/cold).
Apposition	Two words or phrases positioned next to each other that refer to the same thing. Typically noun phrases, the second noun phrase gives more information about the first.

- This is <u>my friend</u>, <u>Sally</u>.
- <u>The house</u>, <u>the first that we viewed</u>, was our favourite.

Article	A type of determiner. There are two types of article: the definite article (<u>the</u>) and the indefinite articles (<u>a</u>/<u>an</u>).
Auxiliary verb	A type of verb used in front of a lexical verb to modify its meaning. Modal verbs are a type of auxiliary verb, but the primary auxiliary verbs are <u>be</u>, <u>do</u> and <u>have</u>.

- Zara <u>was</u> training for a marathon.
- Grandad <u>does</u> enjoy his garden.
- I<u>'ve</u> just thought of a great idea.

(Note that these verbs can also be main – or lexical – verbs: I <u>did</u> my homework even though I <u>was</u> hungry and <u>had</u> a headache.)

Auxiliary verbs are used to make other verb forms, such as the progressive and the perfect forms, as well as the passive.

- I <u>am</u> singing in the choir. (The verb 'be' is used in the progressive form.)
- Sally <u>had</u> wanted to go to Australia since she was a child. (The verb 'have' is used in the perfect form.)
- Our team <u>was</u> defeated on Saturday. (The verb 'be' is used in the passive.)

Cataphoric reference	A cohesive feature in which a word (typically a pronoun) or group of words refers forwards to someone or something mentioned later.

- Although <u>she</u> is only five, <u>Joy</u> already knows her times tables.

Clause   Part of a sentence typically containing a subject, a verb and any additional words or phrases that complete the meaning. Clauses can be main or subordinate.

- <u>Black rhino numbers have slightly increased in recent years</u>. (The main clause is underlined.)
- <u>While they remain an endangered species</u>, black rhino numbers have slightly increased in recent years. (The subordinate clause is underlined.)

Cohesion   The way a text is woven together, typically through the use of devices that operate as signposts for the reader, signalling how different parts of a text relate to each other.

Collocation   A string of words commonly used together in a particular way (<u>fish and chips</u> rather than <u>chips and fish</u>).

Compound   A compound word is a word formed by joining two words together (<u>blackboard</u>, <u>hitchhiking</u>, <u>breathtaking</u>). Some compound words are written as two words or with a hyphen (<u>swimming pool</u>, <u>well-being</u>).

A compound sentence is a sentence that consists of two or more independent clauses (Bill runs marathons, but Alison is training for a triathlon).

Complex sentence   A sentence that contains at least one main clause and at least one subordinate clause. Although this is an established grammatical term, it can give the impression that the meaning conveyed by the sentence is complex, which is not necessarily the case (I went to bed because I was tired).

Conditional clause   Conditionals deal with possible situations and their consequences. They are typically introduced by the subordinating conjunctions <u>if</u> or <u>unless</u>.

- <u>If you tidy your bedroom</u>, you can go swimming later.
- We can't pay for this trip <u>unless we save more money</u>.

Conjunction   A word that joins words, phrases or clauses. There are two types: co-ordinating conjunctions (e.g. <u>and</u>, <u>or</u>, <u>but</u>) and subordinating conjunctions (e.g. <u>because</u>, <u>if</u>, <u>although</u>).

Contracted form   The compression of two or more words into one, with the omitted letter(s) replaced by an apostrophe (can't, shouldn't, we've).

Co-ordination   Co-ordinated clauses have the same grammatical status as each other (either main or subordinate, but not mixed). They are typically joined by a co-ordinating conjunction.

- Joe wanted to see a film <u>or</u> go for a meal, <u>but</u> it was too late.
- We decided to stay in because we were tired <u>and</u> also because it was raining.

Words and phrases can also be co-ordinated.

- Mel <u>and</u> Kate met at university.
- Would you like a mug of coffee <u>or</u> a pot of tea?

Declarative	A clause type that's typically used to give (or declare) information. We tend to refer to these as statements.

- The boat was listing dangerously.
- The team scored the winning goal in the final minute.

Deixis	Associated with spoken language, deictic features depend for their meaning on the immediacy of a shared context, typically to help a speaker to orientate the listener.

- I'd like two of <u>these</u>, please.
- Did you see <u>that</u> programme last night?

Determiner	A word that specifies (or determines) a noun. It comes before the noun, and (in an expanded noun phrase) before any adjectives or nouns that may also form part of the noun phrase.

- <u>my</u> rusty old bike
- <u>that</u> new film
- <u>some</u> cream cakes

Determiners include the following:

- articles (<u>the</u> book, <u>an</u> apple)
- quantifiers (<u>all</u> pupils, <u>some</u> teachers, <u>every</u> school)
- possessives (<u>my</u> job, <u>our</u> mission)
- demonstratives (<u>this</u> outfit, <u>those</u> children)
- interrogatives (<u>which</u> chapter? <u>whose</u> coat?)
- the genitive – sometimes referred to as the possessive –'s (<u>Sarah's</u> car, <u>my parents'</u> house)

Some grammarians also treat numerals as determiners (<u>two</u> cars, <u>fifty-five</u> people).

Dialect	A form of language associated with a particular geographical region or social group, including regional, non-Standard dialects as well as Standard English (which is also a dialect, albeit not linked to any particular geographical region).
Directive	A pragmatic rather than grammatical term, encompassing instructions, advice and commands. Polite directives can use the declarative form (You can come in now) or the interrogative form (Would you like to sit down?), although they are more typically associated with the imperative form (Sit down, please).
Discourse marker	Typically associated with spoken language, these are words that act as signposts to the listener, signalling the beginning or the end of an exchange, or indicating that the speaker is ready to move on to a new topic.

- <u>Right</u>, what's this all about?
- <u>Well then</u>, I'll see you next week.

Ellipsis	The omission of words – typically in spoken language – where the meaning is clear from the shared context.

- Sorry – can't stop. Speak later. (I'm sorry – I can't stop. I'll speak to you later.)
- Flat battery – need to charge it. (I've got a flat battery – I need to charge it.)

Ellipsis dots (. . .) can be used in writing to indicate where words have been omitted or to suggest a 'trailing away', indicating uncertainty, suspense or a cliff hanger . . .

Etymology	The study of word origins and the way word meanings have changed over time
Exclamative	A phrase or clause type typically used to express strong emotion.

- What a brilliant match!
- How upsetting that was!

Finite verb	A verb which indicates tense. (Also see 'non-finite'.)

- He <u>swims</u> every day.
- She <u>swam</u> every day on holiday.

Gerund	A verb ending in –ing that functions as a noun.

- <u>Cycling</u> is not permitted on the pavement.
- <u>Swimming</u> is great exercise.
- No <u>running</u> in the corridor!

Grapheme	A unit of the writing system, typically a letter or group of letters, that represents a phoneme.
Head	The key word in a phrase. For example, the head of a noun phrase is the single noun that is modified by the other words in the noun phrase.

- that rusty old <u>van</u> by the side of the road
- the first <u>day</u> of spring

Historic present	A particular use of the present tense to refer to past time, typically in oral narratives and anecdotes.

- So she <u>comes</u> into the shop and she <u>starts</u> talking to me . . .

Homograph	A word that has the same spelling as another word, but a different meaning and pronunciation.

- The argument developed into a terrific <u>row</u>!
- You need to <u>row</u> towards the bank.

Homonym	A word that has the same pronunciation and spelling as another word, but a different meaning.

- I opened a <u>bank</u> account.
- I sat by the river <u>bank</u>.
- Don't <u>bank</u> on it!

Hombophone	A word that has the same pronunciation as another word, but a different meaning and spelling.

- sore/saw
- aisle/isle
- threw/through

Imperative A 'mood' that expresses directive meaning such as a command. The 'bare' imperative is formed from the base form of the verb without the infinitive 'to'.

- <u>Sit</u> down!
- <u>Look</u> at this . . .
- Please <u>stop</u> that.

Indicative A 'mood' that expresses factual meaning. This is the most commonly used of the three 'moods' (the other two 'moods' being the imperative and the subjunctive).

Infinitive The base form of a verb, often preceded by 'to'. The infinitive form is non-finite. It might be helpful to think of it as the 'name' of the verb (e.g. <u>to think</u>).

Inflection The way a word changes its shape to reflect a different grammatical meaning. An inflected ending can indicate a change of tense (wait/wait<u>ed</u>) or number (flower/flower<u>s</u>), but words, particularly irregular verbs, can be inflected in other ways too (buy/bought).

Interjection A word that expresses strong emotion or surprise.

- Yuk!
- Ouch!
- Wow . . .

Interrogative A clause type that's typically used to request information. We tend to refer to these as questions.

Irregular verb A verb that doesn't conform to the regular inflected form, typically in the simple past and the –ed form (past participle). There are many irregular verbs in English.

- He swam (rather than 'swimmed') twenty lengths.
- I bought (rather than 'buyed') a new winter coat.

Lexical verb A type of verb that is not an auxiliary or a modal verb. Sometimes referred to as a 'content' verb, it typically depicts actions, events and states.

- Harry <u>rode</u> his bike to football practice.
- We <u>trudged</u> along the footpath until we <u>arrived</u>, exhausted, at the hostel.
- We <u>remained</u> good friends.

Main clause A clause that is not dependent for its meaning on another clause, but makes sense on its own. When demarcated by a capital letter and full stop (or other end punctuation), it becomes a sentence.

- The black rhino is an endangered species.
- As a result of conservation efforts, black rhino numbers are slowly increasing although the threat from poaching remains great.

Minor sentence

A word, phrase or clause that functions as a sentence, but doesn't contain a main clause. Interjections fall into this category. Minor sentences are frequently used in advertising and journalism for impact and concision.

- Hello.
- For sale.
- No problem!
- Snow havoc!

Modal verb

A particular type of auxiliary verb that expresses an attitude such as possibility, certainty, necessity or ability. There are nine core modal verbs: <u>can</u>, <u>could</u>, <u>may</u>, <u>might</u>, <u>must</u>, <u>shall</u>, <u>should</u>, <u>will</u> and <u>would</u>. Some grammarians also recognise <u>ought to</u> and <u>used to</u> as semi-modals (or marginal modals).

Modification

The addition of extra detail before (pre-modification) or after (post-modification) a word, phrase or clause.

Mood

The writer's attitude as indicated by the verb form. There are three 'moods': the indicative mood, which expresses factual meaning; the imperative mood, which expresses directive meaning; and the subjunctive mood, which expresses unfulfilled or desired states, events or actions as well as compulsion or necessity.

Morpheme

The smallest grammatical unit that carries meaning in a word.

- The word 'disagreement' consists of three morphemes: dis + agree + ment.
- The word 'classrooms' also consists of three morphemes: class + room + s.

Morphology

In terms of linguistics, morphology refers to the study of the form and structure of words. In particular, it refers to the way words can be changed by inflection and the addition of affixes.

Nominal clause

A clause that functions as a noun or noun phrase, sometimes referred to as a noun clause. Like a noun or noun phrase, it can be the subject of a sentence and it can be replaced by a pronoun.

- <u>Learning to swim</u> is the best thing I've ever done.
- <u>How the police ever managed to solve that case</u> was a mystery to me.

Nominalisation

The formation of a noun from another word class – usually a verb or an adjective.

- The <u>disappearance</u> of the money caused us considerable <u>concern</u>. (with nominalisation)
- We were <u>concerned</u> that the money had <u>disappeared</u>. (without nominalisation)

Non-finite verb

A non-tensed verb, formed in one of three ways:

- The –ed form (sometimes called the past participle or the –ed participle)
- The –ing form (sometimes called the present participle or the –ing participle)
- The infinitive form (the base form of the verb preceded by 'to')

A non-finite clause is a type of subordinate clause that is introduced by a non-finite (or non-tensed) verb.

- <u>Running late for his meeting</u>, Bob decided to hail a taxi.
- <u>Dazed by all the attention</u>, the toddler started to cry.
- <u>To imagine the scene</u>, you must first close your eyes . . .

Noun

A word that names a 'thing', such as <u>book</u>, <u>biscuit</u> or <u>computer</u>. Nouns typically have a singular and a plural form (book/books). They can be modified by determiners (those books, my books) or adjectives (those old books, my favourite books).

Proper nouns name specific things, including people, places and events (<u>Big Ben</u>, <u>Cardiff</u>, the <u>Olympic Games</u>).

Abstract nouns name feelings, qualities, ideas or concepts (such as <u>excitement</u>, <u>generosity</u>, or <u>peace</u>).

Collective nouns (such as <u>staff</u>, <u>committee</u>, or <u>team</u>) can take either a plural or a singular verb, depending on whether the writer wishes to emphasise the collective group (singular) or the individuals within it (plural).

Noun phrase

A phrase with a noun or pronoun as its 'head' modified (or expanded) in some way, e.g. by a determiner, an adjective, another noun, a preposition phrase or a relative clause.

- a freshly dug <u>molehill</u> at the bottom of my garden
- the crumbling <u>ruin</u> perched on the edge of the cliff

Object

See 'subject'.

Parenthesis

A word or group of words inserted into a sentence as a kind of afterthought, usually punctuated by a pair of brackets, dashes or commas. (The term 'parentheses' can also be used to refer to a pair of brackets.)

Participle

The –ing and –ed non-finite verb forms, sometimes referred to as the present and past participles.

Passive voice

The less frequently used 'voice', whereby the subject of the verb is the recipient of – or the one affected by – the action. The passive tends to place less focus on the agent (which is sometimes omitted) and more on the actual action or event. The passive is typically formed from the appropriate tense of the verb 'be' plus the –ed form (past participle) of the main verb.

- The vase was broken by Sam. (The active equivalent would be <u>Sam broke the vase</u>.)
- The trees were felled by the gale-force winds. (The active equivalent would be <u>The gale-force winds felled the trees</u>.)

Perfect

A verb form that enables the writer to indicate that a completed action still has current relevance.

The present perfect is formed from 'have' plus the –ed form (past participle) of a main verb and indicates an action or event that started in the past but continues in (or continues to be relevant to) the present time.

- We <u>have waited</u> in this queue for hours.

The past perfect is formed from 'had' plus the –ed form (past participle) of a main verb and indicates an action that started in the past and continued to another point in the past.

- I <u>had</u> always <u>wanted</u> to go to Australia.

Phoneme   The smallest distinct unit of sound in a word. In writing, phonemes are represented by graphemes.

Phrase   A group of words acting as a grammatical unit and typically forming part of a clause. There are different types of phrase, such as noun phrase and preposition phrase.

Prefix   A letter or letters attached to the beginning of a word to change its meaning or to make a new word (<u>mal</u>practice). Some prefixes can form a word's antonym (<u>un</u>necessary).

Preposition   A word that indicates the relationship between things, people or events, typically (but not necessarily) in terms of time or place.

- We arrived <u>before</u> lunch.
- Philip searched <u>behind</u> the sofa.
- Would you like to come <u>with</u> me?
- He looks just <u>like</u> his father.

Preposition phrase   A phrase with a preposition as its 'head'.

- <u>under</u> the stairs
- <u>without</u> mayonnaise
- <u>after</u> a long and tiring journey <u>across</u> the Atlantic

Preterite   Another name for the simple past.

Progressive   A verb form that indicates an action in progress, either in the past or the present tense. It is formed from the appropriate tense of the auxiliary verb 'be' plus the –ing form of a main (lexical) verb.

- I <u>am singing</u> in the choir.
- We <u>were</u> only <u>joking</u>.

Pronoun   A word that stands in (like a substitute) for a noun or noun phrase.

Pronouns help to avoid unnecessary repetition and so aid cohesion in writing.

- <u>Michael</u> looked out of the window. <u>He</u> was worried.
- Simi picked up <u>the heavy wooden box</u> and put <u>it</u> on the table.

There are different types of pronoun:

- Personal pronouns refer to specific people or things. They have both subject forms (I, you, he, she, it, we, you, they) and object forms (me, you, him, her, it, us, you, them).
- Possessive pronouns indicate ownership (or possession). They are classed as either possessive pronouns (mine, yours, his, hers, ours, yours, theirs) or possessive determiners (my, your, his, her, its, our, your, their). <u>Its</u> can be used as a possessive determiner (the dog is wagging <u>its</u> tail), but not as a possessive pronoun.

- Reflexive pronouns (myself, yourself, himself, herself, itself, ourselves, yourselves, themselves) refer back to (or reflect) the subject of the clause (<u>I</u> corrected <u>myself</u>).

- Interrogative pronouns (who, whose, whom, what, whatever, which, whichever) are used to ask questions.

- Demonstrative pronouns (this, that, these, those) are used to 'point' to things.

- Relative pronouns (who, whom, whose, which, that) are used to introduce relative clauses.

- Reciprocal pronouns (each other, one another) are used to indicate actions or feelings that are reciprocated.

- Indefinite pronouns (e.g. anybody, everyone, nothing, something) refer to people or things in a less specific way.

Register	The specific language used in particular social contexts and by specific groups or professions (e.g. legal, medical or scientific) or the use of more formal or informal language dependent on context and audience.
Relative clause	A type of subordinate clause that post-modifies a noun, a noun phrase, a clause or a whole sentence.

- the book <u>that I want</u>
- the train, <u>which was already full</u>
- the reason <u>why she left</u>

Sometimes the relative pronoun is omitted altogether.

- the book <u>I want</u>
- the reason <u>she left</u>

Relative clauses can be defining or non-defining (see Chapter 2).

Relative pronoun	A type of pronoun used to introduce a relative clause (who, whom, whose, which, that). The relative adverbs (when, where, why) can also introduce a relative clause.
Root word	The smallest possible word once any affixes have been removed, e.g. inter<u>nation</u>al. A root word is distinct from a base word, which may already include an affix, although the terms tend to be used interchangeably.
Sentence	A group of words that forms a complete unit with no grammatical links to the words before and after. It typically contains at least one main clause. In writing, a sentence is demarcated by a capital letter and a full stop. Sentences can function as statements, questions, exclamations or commands.
Simple forms	A verb form used to indicate the simple present or simple past. The simple present is formed from the base form of the verb (the –s form is used to form the third person singular). The simple past is formed from the –ed form of the verb, although irregular verbs take other forms.

Simple sentence   A sentence that consists of one single clause. Although this is an established grammatical term, it can give the impression that the meaning conveyed by the sentence is simple, which is not necessarily the case (The teacher carefully manoeuvred his brand-new sports car into the very last space in the school car park). For this reason, some grammarians prefer the term 'single-clause sentence'.

Standard English   The dialect that is generally used for formal purposes in speech and writing, carrying a clear element of social and academic prestige.

Subject   In the active voice, the person or thing that performs the action of the verb. The subject and verb must agree in terms of number and person. In a declarative clause, the subject comes before the verb.

- <u>Jimmy</u> is peeling an apple.
- <u>The dogs</u> chase the ball.
- Last night, <u>I</u> watched a really good film with my friends.

Some clauses also have an object. The object typically comes after the verb and might be said to be affected by the action of the verb. Objects can be direct or indirect.

- Jimmy is peeling <u>an apple</u>.
- The dogs chase <u>the ball</u>.
- Last night, I watched <u>a really good film</u> with my friends.

Subjunctive   A 'mood' that expresses unfulfilled or desired states, events or actions as well as compulsion or necessity. It is associated with very formal – and sometimes archaic – writing. It can be formed in more than one way.

The present (or mandative) subjunctive uses the base form of the verb rather than the usual –s ending in the third person singular.

- The governors insist that the headteacher <u>take</u> a holiday.
- I demand that the firm <u>compensate</u> me in full.

The past (or 'were') subjunctive takes the form 'were' (rather than 'was') in the first and third person singular.

- If I <u>were</u> you, I would reconsider my options.
- Tom looked as though he <u>were</u> about to burst into tears.

Subordination   Subordinate clauses cannot make a complete sentence on their own, but contribute their meaning to a main (or independent) clause. They can be finite or non-finite. Finite subordinate clauses are introduced by a subordinating conjunction.

- <u>Whenever we go on holiday</u>, it always rains.
- The idea <u>that I wanted her job</u> is completely absurd.
- Bake the pastry <u>until it's crisp</u>.
- We didn't know <u>when you were coming</u>.

Suffix   A letter or letters attached to the end of a word to change its meaning or to make a different word class (honour<u>able</u>, encourage<u>ment</u>, liquid<u>ise</u>).

Synonym	A word that has the same (or similar) meaning to another word (cold/chilly/freezing).
Tense	The use of a particular verb form to indicate the time frame of an event or action.
Verb	A word that tells us what someone or something is doing, such as <u>hit</u>, <u>hate</u> or <u>be</u>. There are three types of verb: lexical, auxiliary and modal.
	With the exception of modal verbs, verbs have a past and present tense and can take different forms.

- The <u>base form</u> is also referred to as the infinitive form (watch/to watch, sleep/to sleep, be/to be).
- The <u>–s form</u> is used to form the simple present in the third person singular (she laughs, it rains, Jack sighs).
- The <u>–ed form</u> is used to form the simple past (they laughed, it rained, we sighed) and the –ed participle, which is used to form the present and past perfect (they have laughed, it has rained, Jack had sighed) as well as the passive voice (the window was smashed).
- The <u>–ing form</u> is used to form the present and past progressive (we were laughing, Jack is sighing, it was raining).

Verb phrase	A phrase with a lexical (or content) verb as its 'head'. The term 'complex verb phrase' is sometimes used when auxiliary and modal verbs combine with a lexical verb in a longer chain of verbs.

- We'<u>d been going</u> every year until . . .
- They <u>could have seen</u> the film . . .
- It <u>had been raining</u> all week . . .
- The company <u>was being bought</u> by competitors . . .

Word class	A group of words that function in the same way, such as nouns, adjectives or determiners. Word class can sometimes depend on context:

- I was afraid of water before I learnt to swim. (before = conjunction)
- I won't be there before 6pm. (before = preposition)

Word root	As distinct from 'root words', a word root relates to a word's origin and its link to the word's meaning. For example, the words <u>attract</u>, <u>extraction</u> and <u>intractable</u> all come from the root 'tract', meaning to drag or pull.

Further reading

Isabel L. Beck, Margaret G. McKeown and Linda Kucan, *Bringing Words to Life: Robust Vocabulary Instruction*, second edition (Guilford Press, 2013).

Isabel L. Beck, Margaret G. McKeown and Richard C. Omanson, 'The Effects and Uses of Diverse Vocabulary Instructional Techniques', in Margaret G. McKeown and Mary E. Curtis (eds), *The Nature of Vocabulary Acquisition*, pp. 147–163 (Erlbaum, 1987).

Ronald Carter and Michael McCarthy, *Cambridge Grammar of English* (Cambridge University Press, 2010).

David Crystal, *Rediscover Grammar* (Longman, 2004).

David Crystal, *Making a Point* (Profile Books, 2015).

Department for Children, Schools and Families, *Getting Going: Generating, Shaping and Developing Ideas in Writing* (DCSF, 2008).

Robert MacNeil, *Wordstruck: A Memoir* (Random House, 1989).

Robert MacNeil, *Qualifications and Curriculum Authority, Introducing the Grammar of Talk* (QCA, 2004).

John Seely, *Oxford A–Z of Grammar & Punctuation* (Oxford University Press, 2004).

Jo Shackleton, *Grammar Survival for Primary Teachers: A Practical Toolkit* (Routledge, 2017).

Steven A. Stahl and William E. Nagy, *Teaching Word Meanings* (Routledge, 2006).

R. L. Trask, *Penguin Guide to Punctuation* (Penguin Books, 1997).

Peter Trudgill, 'Standard English: What it Isn't', in Tony Bex and Richard J. Watts (eds), *Standard English: The Widening Debate*, pp. 117–128 (Routledge, 1999).